MW00915058

RAJI RAJAGOPALAN

Daring to be Different: Stories and Tips from a Woman Leader in Tech

Kishor,

It's good to get to know you. Best wishes in all your endeavors!

Raji

First published by Raji Rajagopalan 2022

Copyright © 2022 by Raji Rajagopalan

All rights reserved. No part of this publication may be reproduced, stored or transmitted in any form or by any means, electronic, mechanical, photocopying, recording, scanning, or otherwise without written permission from the publisher. It is illegal to copy this book, post it to a website, or distribute it by any other means without permission.

First edition

This book was professionally typeset on Reedsy.
Find out more at reedsy.com

Contents

I

Part One

Beginnings

1

Introduction

Picture a scrawny five-year-old girl standing alone in a dark room by a small window. Shafts of early morning light are slashing through the window and spilling onto the floor. The room smells of old blankets and termites. The girl, her large chocolate-brown eyes unblinking, can hear her stomach growl. But she is paying no attention to that low roar. Her heart is thumping. She is standing on tiptoes and gazing out at a procession on the street.

She can see her brother, six years older than her, at the head of the procession. His head is hanging low, and he is dressed in a dhoti - a loose white robe - from his waist down. The little girl then sees her father. Her father is holding on to one end of a wooden plank. A garlanded woman is lying on the plank. She is the center of the procession.

The girl realizes, with a spasm in her heart, that the supine woman is her mother. "What is happening to my mother?" she wonders, "Where are they taking her? Why is this room locked?" Questions froth in her head like seawater in a cyclone. Tears mist her eyes. The girl stands there, just staring, until the last person in the procession has left her sight.

That little girl by the window, in a small, dusty Indian town, was me. The procession was my mother's last journey, to the crematorium. It was one of the first memories of my life.

That day had dawned like any other. The brisk hum of morning life in my home had kicked in. My grandmother had just finished boiling fragrant milk in our windowless kitchen. My brother was sitting cross-legged on the cold floor, doing his math sums. My father had drawn a bucket of water from our borewell to take with him to our outdoor bathroom. My mother sat down on our swing, with a little stainless-steel cup of steaming, sweet coffee in her hand. It was right after that, after she took a few sips of her drink, that she clutched her chest. She cried out for my grandma. "My chest hurts," she said. She slumped back on the swing and lost consciousness.

A few minutes later, she drew her last breath.

It is unclear to me, to this day, what was the exact cause of my mother's untimely death. But one thing is for certain. My life became chaotic and upside down the day she died. My father became overwhelmed. Being a single dad is never easy and being a father to a girl with no woman to support him was doubly harder. While I have seen no one that handled the death of the love of their life better, there was a deep sadness now in my father's life. My brother became hard to manage. He was a stubborn child who had clung to our mom like ivy to an old wall. His sturdy wall had crashed, and he was now withering away. My father's gaze had to be centered on him. It became a struggle to get my brother to eat. He buried his little face into his musty pillows and cried till his eyelids swelled up like balloons. He refused to go to school, refused to do homework. My father spent a lot of time with him.

I observed all of this, silently, trying to make sense of our new lives. My grandma – my father's mother – came to help us. But she was an old woman with old-fashioned ideas. My father felt he could not give me the love and the care I needed by raising me himself alongside his old mother. He decided to find relatives to care for me - capable female relatives who could guide me well.

After that decision, for most of my childhood, I lived in relative care. That is, I was cared for by my extended family, whomever could afford to take me in at that moment. I moved from one relative's house to another, from one school to another. There was never enough money. If we bought apples, for example, we would divide our share, and no one would get a second portion. When I came of age, I used cotton rags to stanch my menstrual blood because we couldn't afford sanitary pads. I conserved paper and ink by doing my math on a black slate with a piece of white, powdery chalk. Don't get me wrong, I was never poor. Having lived in India, I understand what true poverty is. But we were not wealthy either. We were middle class, raised with the values of lower middle class. The lights had to be turned off promptly as you left a room. We watched TV at one neighbor's house, used another neighbor's fridge, and our neighbors used our telephone. We went out to restaurants once a year, maybe twice.

My relatives did their best, undeniably. Some of my family truly cared for me and felt a duty to look after a motherless child. But there were a lot of prejudices too. People saw hierarchies everywhere. The caste system reached its ugly, stinky fingers into our lives every day. Colorism was all too real. I was told I wasn't pretty enough, that my brown skin was too dark for most bright clothes I loved to wear. I was asked to take my nose out of my books – like a girl should – and learn to cook and clean. Becoming someone's loving wife was supposed to be my destiny. Superstition made people fear widows, cats, people from lower castes, and frightful gods. I noticed the abominable prejudices around me, and I actively rebelled against some. I built a reputation in the family for being a brat with a big mouth. As a result, every few years, I would become too much for one relative and therefore handed off to another one.

My challenging beginnings, where I was tossed like a hot lump of coal from one hand to another, in a society riddled with antiquated ideas, undoubtedly left a mark on me. Every time my father would visit me, and then wave me goodbye, I would feel my heart shrivel. I loved my dad, and I knew that he loved me. Everything else around me was tinged with uncertainty. So, whenever my dad left my side physically, I felt like all the love around me was getting sucked out of the room. I grew up fearing that I would be abandoned at any tick of the clock. I developed distance from people, never letting myself grow attached to anyone. Or anything, really. I knew nothing was permanent – there was always the next relative's house around the corner. But this instability also strangely taught me many things that would later help me in my professional life. I learned to stand up for myself. I learned to be nimble and resilient. I became determined, with a will of iron. I learned to build relationships quickly. But more than anything, I learned to accept my circumstances in life, while at the same time working ferociously to break free of them.

With resolve, persistence, and some good luck, I managed to break free of my broken beginnings. I became a technologist and moved to North America in 1999. I became an engineer at a large software company in Seattle. I climbed the corporate ladder, rung after rung, becoming a Partner (a level just below Vice President) at the company in a dozen years. As I did so, I learned lesson after lesson. I faced setbacks: feeling like a fraud, being a misfit, being unable to get my voice out in rooms full of people that did not look like me. I developed mantras and techniques to guide me. I started mentoring people in my network. I listened to story after story.

It was always the same. Many people - especially people of color, women, immigrants, introverts - in high-octane professions told me that they faced similar challenges in their workplace. They asked me if I had advice on how to deal with difficult people, how to calm meeting nerves, how to get their voice out, how to silence their inner critic, how to make good career decisions, how to train their fear of public speaking, how to live a fulfilling life, and so on. They asked me how I got my success, as a woman, as a person of color, in technology. I started sharing the lessons I had learned with these folks. Then I started writing about these topics in my blog. Folks loved what I wrote and found the advice concrete, inspiring, relevant, and valuable. They wanted more.

That was how I conceived this book. This book is a compilation of some of my blog posts most relevant to a career in technology, with additional thoughts that I have never published before. Many tech companies want to increase the diversity in their ranks. I have personally been involved in initiatives to do so at my company. I have realized that many young people that are underrepresented in our workplace are hungry for guidance. I know that because I mentor and manage many such folks. I am one of those folks. We work hard and have sturdy skills, and yet we find several hurdles in our

6

path to success. Some of these hurdles are laid out in front of us by our culture – our workplace culture and our societal culture. Some, though, are hurdles we build for ourselves. To vault over these hurdles, wouldn't it be great to have some guidance? Not just any guidance, but guidance from someone who has been there and done that, someone who has fought against many barriers in life and become successful? Wouldn't it be great to learn how to go from 0 to 1, so to speak in computer jargon, in our work life?

In this book, I talk about my experience with my own hurdles and how I conquered them. I am still a work in progress, most definitely, but I have also gathered principles, skills, and tactics over the years to combat our tallest hurdles. I have shared this advice with the people I have coached and mentored. These are tips that have worked in practice, for me and for others. My goal in recounting them here is to encourage you to try them in your own life. My hope is that they will work for you too.

I plan to organize this book in two parts. Part 1 will center on stories from my early life, especially the ones that touch upon prejudices against women and the many challenges that folks from underprivileged backgrounds face. The idea behind some of my early stories is to help you become familiar with my origins, the setbacks I faced early on, and the lessons I carried away from those experiences that helped me in my career. This part will be shorter than the second part, which will center on stories from my professional life, including my journey into technology, with concrete advice that answers many common career challenges.

Each chapter will deal with a specific topic. First, you need to **show up and find opportunities**. The chapters on being audacious, dealing with the fear of the unknown, and being open to reinventing yourself can help you with that. In a workplace that is so diverse, and so unlike your own background, you need to build **emotional intelligence** skills. The chapters on facing meeting jitters, dealing with envy, subduing the harmful stories in your head, letting go of toxic situations, working with difficult people, and understanding meeting dynamics by getting on the balcony speak to that.

Another set of skills vital for your career growth is **communication**. The chapters on writing and storytelling discuss how you can develop these skills.

Lastly, the chapters on the secret of success, how to do well on the first days of any job, work lessons from a superhero, how ambitious one should be, and how to lead a fulfilling life can help you **better your productivity, increase your performance, and leave a good legacy behind.**

All of these are topics that have come up repeatedly in my mentoring conversations. I have written and spoken about a number of these topics before – in my blog and in my various speaking engagements. My audience has repeatedly told me how the advice and the stories have helped them. But I have never put them all together like I have done in this book.

Over the years, we have made lengthy strides toward equality in the workplace. We have several women leaders in top national offices around the world. In January 2021, we welcomed our first woman, first black, first person of South Asian descent into the office of Vice Presidency of the United States. In tech companies, diversity representation percentages are inching up steadily. Still, there is much work to do. A lot of that work involves culture change. Corporate leaders will need to expand their radars for recruitment and establish or augment programs for retaining and growing diverse talent. Some work, however, has to do with the individual. How one can learn to navigate their career successfully. That is what this book is for.

Today, I am an Engineering Director at a large software company, managing teams of developers across four continents. I speak at conferences and have worked with fifty entrepreneurs to bootstrap their social enterprises. I mentor young professionals. I have a loving, equal partner who supports me. Despite what looks like a wondrous life on the outside, I carry scars that are invisible, and I deal with those scars every day. Our lives are seldom perfect. If there is one thing that I want you to take away from this book, it is that success is possible despite the challenges that life throws at you. There is quiet after stormy nights. No matter what you are going through, there is hope and room for grand dreams.

2

An early migrant

What uncertainty in life can teach you about work

My husband lived in the same house, with the same three people, for the first twenty years of his life. He went to the same school from kindergarten until college. His mom worked as a teacher, a job that made her feet hurt and her voice hoarse at the end of long days. Despite that, she religiously woke up at five in the morning every day to pack fresh, home-cooked lunches for her kids. My husband spent afternoons with aunts who coddled him. He went to the beach on the weekends with his uncle and cousins, where they ate ice cream cones or slices of green mango sprinkled with chili and salt. My husband's family was his rock, his foundation. His early years were filled with love.

For me, it was something altogether different. After my mother died, and my father decided he couldn't keep me with him, I became somewhat of a wanderer in my life. I lived in seven different houses with six different families for the first twenty years of my life. I lived with different people, each house smelling and sounding different.

The first house I lived in was our ancestral home in a tiny, quiet town called Kumbakonam. Kumbakonam is a South Indian town famous for its temples. In this town, you find the freshest spinach, the sweetest water, the juiciest mangoes, and the purest milk in the length and breadth of my home state. At least, that is what the residents of Kumbakonam liked to say. The town boasts a ribbon of a river called Cauvery, with trees laden with leaves drooping over its water, giving the water a cool moss-green color.

The house that I lived in, typical of traditional houses in that region, was deeper than it was wide. It looked like the body of an earthworm, each segment carefully laid out next to the other, attached back to front. You could start walking from the entrance, in a straight line for minutes, deeper and deeper into the heart of the house, until you reached the lush backyard, thick with crepe jasmine shrubs and coconut trees. It had multiple open courtyards, a dank kitchen with a wood burning stove and stone grinding equipment. It had a large indoor swing - the swing on which my mother drew her last breath - made of wooden plank and iron chains. It had a dark bedroom with a small window from which I glimpsed my mother's journey to the crematorium. I lived in this house for the first five years of my life. After my mother died, my father could not bear to live in the same house. In fact, he could not bear to live in the same town. We moved to Chennai.

My next house, where I lived with my grandma and my dad, was a flat on the third floor of a building in Chennai. I remember only a few things about this house. There was an Asoka tree outside our bedroom, where a sparrow had meticulously built a nest out of twigs and cotton. There was a tiny shack a few doors from us, where I would often buy sugary, fruit-flavored popsicles for just a few *paise* I had squirreled away from my family.

There was a government hospital opposite our flat, with big signs painted in black and red paint on its façade, advertising birth control. There was a community garbage heap nearby that reeked of rotten fruits, blood, and excrement. Waste from the hospital and the community was routinely dumped there. Little boys in badly fitting shorts would clamber over the mounds of trash, a jute sack thrown over their shoulders, looking for paper, plastic, cans – anything they could sell for a little money. Stray dogs and fat pigs had babies on it. Occasionally, trash was set on fire, and the smoke and the smell seeped into our clothes, under our nails, into our hair, into our skin.

My grandmother was a no-nonsense woman and an indefatigable task master. She expected a lot out of herself and a lot out of me. She wanted to raise me - a motherless child who was suddenly her responsibility - into a charming wife and a dutiful daughter-in-law. I would grow up to admire my grandma's strong will and sheer strength, but we were constantly at odds. She wanted me to learn to clean the house and fold the laundry. I - strangely for a child, but not too strangely for a rebellious child - wanted to study instead.

I was quite the match for my strong-willed grandma. I was not inclined to be a silent motherless child, bearing all my pain by being cocooned inside an armor of silence. I was cantankerous. My grandma would yank my books off my hand and shout at me to mind the laundry. I would shout back at her, in my tiny six-year-old voice that I wanted to study, just like my brother was doing at that exact moment. My grandma would forbid me to wear skirts that stopped above my shins. When I asked her to buy me shampoo to wash my hair with, she would just shake her head. Western ideas were corrupting me, she would say. Like a good Tamil girl, I should wear full skirts and use herbs to wash my hair. I would protest that my classmates were laughing at my greasy hair.

It was in the middle of this open war between us that my first career lesson would emerge. One of my aunts, Sundari, was visiting us from Delhi. She was the only woman in my family that had a career. Every other woman I grew up with was a homemaker, partially educated and with no desire or means to work. This aunt was different. She was independent and fierce. When she was visiting me, one day as were sitting on our balcony swatting at the million mosquitoes around us, I told her about my struggles with grandma. I was in tears. I explained to her how embarrassed I was at school, how badly my hair stank. My aunt listened to me patiently. She then went into the house. When she got back, she had a little red cloth purse in her hand. She took out a hundred-rupee note from it and stuffed it into my palm. "Don't keep fighting this fight every day," she told me, "Go get yourself some shampoo packets and use them - quietly".

I didn't know it at the time – though I certainly internalized it – that that interaction with my aunt was profound for my career. It taught me that I need to look at my problems from all angles and try to reframe them. The problem, in this case, was not that my grandma was mean to me. The problem was that I didn't have the independence and the means to get what I wanted. I needed to speak up to people that could help. To allies, and to people with influence. Haranguing my grandmother – not an ally in this case – was no use. But talking to my aunt? Now, that helped tremendously. I needed to solve my own problems, quietly, and creatively. I needed to stand up for my rights, but not fight the same fight every day and expect a different result.

In time, my dad began to suspect that all was not okay between me and grandma. It dawned on him that I needed the care of a younger, more modern woman - a mother figure. My mother's sister agreed to take me in. Her house, back in Kumbakonam, was built with ancient stones and had low ceilings and little alcoves for oil lamps. Frogs croaked at night from inside the stone sink in their kitchen. Cockroaches roamed freely, and some even took flight. The routines in this house were so different from what I had become used to in bustling Chennai. Unlike my grandma, the womenfolk here were never rushed. They slept in the afternoon and cooked the rest of the time. At school too, everything was different. New uniforms, new teachers, a new syllabus, new rules, and most importantly, new classmates. I learned that, at home and at school, I had to watch and learn constantly. Everyone was different, and every family had a dozen unspoken rules. I had to understand what made up this new world, and how I could be ok within it. I came to my new schools with a smile on my face and a desire to make friends. I learned to watch, learn, adapt, and build relationships. Another life lesson that I would carry with me into my adult life, when I became an immigrant in two countries and a leader in a field filled with people that didn't look like me.

After two years, I moved again. I do not fully grasp the reasons for this move or the three that followed it, but I know that my dad always had good reasons in his mind. He was a single dad struggling to raise two kids with little help. And of course, I was not an easy child for relatives to care for. While I could swiftly adapt to new surroundings, I had a mind that buzzed like a beehive. I had a mouth on me too. I quibbled with folks whenever I found anything that smelled of injustice, of which there was plenty in my family. I will get to caste and gender equality injustices in due time.

There was also the reality of my being another mouth to feed, an intruder in my relatives' families, someone they now needed to divide their space and food with, someone they needed to buy notebooks and combs and *Hamam* soap for. They tried to accommodate, but often it didn't work out. So, off I went from one home to another, packing up my few things and saying goodbyes to the few kids that were just beginning to become friends.

I sometimes wonder how my life would have been if I had had more stability in my childhood. Would I have found it easier to be a good student? Would I have been happier? I don't know. Growing up, I envied my brother because he got to stay with my dad, while I was thrown around like a hot potato. But in hindsight, my fragmented childhood made me who I am today. In the book *Becoming*, Michelle Obama makes this point beautifully. She says:

Your story is what you have, what you will always have. It is something to own.

My story of my childhood is one of separations, losses, and strife. It is a story that made me fear being abandoned, fear not being loved, and - paradoxically - gave me an unusual level of detachment from family. But I am proud of my story. You cannot make sense of your life looking forward, and I certainly didn't try to when I was a child. Looking back now, I realize a few things. Moving around so much and the constant learning were certainly exhausting. But they also taught me agility, comfort with change, resilience, and the courage to stand up for myself – all important lessons for my career. Until recently, I could not point to any single house and call it home. Unlike my husband, I could not call a city or town "my hometown". I was from everywhere and from nowhere. Every place I have lived in has become a part of me. It has made me who I am, and yet I feel untethered to places and objects. I became a migrant early in my life – not out of choice - and now I will always be one in my heart.

Here are some things to try

We often do not pay attention to the stories that made us. Take some time now and reflect on where you come from, what your origin story is, what made you who you are, and what lessons you have learned through your early years. Your superpowers are hidden within your story.

Some parting thoughts

Speak up when you are unhappy, or when you see a problem.

Own your problems. Be resourceful and creative in finding solutions.

Watch, learn, adapt.

Build relationships.

Learn to rely on yourself.

Be open to and comfortable with change.

Look back on your life to make sense of what you have been through, and what your life has taught you.

No matter what your story is like, reflect on it, learn from it, and be proud of it.

3

A tube of red lipstick

Why you should have a career

A few years ago, I visited my cousin in Toronto. She and her husband had just immigrated to Canada and were living in a one-bedroom apartment on the seventh floor of a building. After we finished lunch the day after I had landed, we sat in her airy living room, white winter sunshine streaming in through her French doors. Like cousins do at reunions, we talked about this and that – growing up in Kumbakonam, the weather, our family's foibles and so on – but finally we landed on the topic of *career*.

My cousin said she was proud of my professional success. She was proud of *me*, she said. The entire family was. I asked her about her own dreams and ambitions. She was a new immigrant with a visa that allowed her to work in her country. She had a graduate degree in Computer Science from a university in India. She was a personable, capable, and hard-working woman. Was she planning to interview? I asked. Does she want to apply to Microsoft or Facebook or any of the other popular tech companies? Can I help?

"No," she told me, "I don't want to do that."

"Why not?" I asked, puzzled.

"I am not as smart as you, Raji," she answered.

"You can't say that" I said, "And it's not being smart or not, it is about learning and trying. How do you even know I am smarter than you?"

We went back and forth on the topic, but she would have none of what I said. She wrongly thought that I was endowed with brains to have a sterling career and she was not. I felt that she was needlessly holding back and psyching herself out. But more concerningly, I felt that she was choosing to step out of a career even before she entered it. She was treating her career as entirely optional, which in my worldview, was entirely flawed.

I felt that my cousin, like a lot of us from strained backgrounds, lacked confidence in herself. She felt safe hanging in the back, being quiet and invisible. She lacked role models that taught her of the possibilities that could be. Growing up, both my cousin and I didn't have anyone that modeled female empowerment and employment for us. Most of the women in our family were homemakers.

Let's start with my mother.

My mother didn't live long – she died when she was thirty-two – but she was remarkable when she was alive. She had liquid brown eyes that were shaped like large almonds. With her small nose, and her narrow jaw, she was a stunning woman. My father had fallen in love with her before he married her, something that was unusual in Indian marriages of their time. My mother was not highly educated though. She finished high school, but after she graduated, her family decided to stop her education. That was in keeping with her time.

Women didn't used to get educated beyond high school in my mother's era. It was a rare woman that had a college degree, and a rarer one with a career. People thought that education for a woman spoiled her. It meant trouble. She could become too dominant in the family, could develop strong opinions. A good bride was a quiet, malleable, and an ignorant one. My mother was smart, there was no doubt about it. But she didn't have the privilege to be educated beyond twelfth grade. The norms just would not have it.

After she married my dad, and my brother was on his way into the world, she realized that she would have to work. My father had an entry-level job at a national bank, and soon - they figured - the family income would not be enough. So, she found herself a job on a factory floor, boxing automobile parts. But that was not a career; it was a way to bring some extra cash into the household. When my father got a better-paying job, my mother simply quit. After a few years, I was born, and my mother never got paid for her work again.

It was worse for my mother's mother. My grandma was born in a tiny village called Ganapathi Agraharam, famous for its breezy rice fields. She was sharp as a scythe. If she had been born in more modern times, she would have gone on to have a college education and do insanely cool things. In her time, though, she was expected to stop school when she started menstruating. My grandma got her first periods when she was in eighth grade. The family conferred on what to do. The girl – my grandma – was just too smart. Even for those backward times, it was unconscionable to stop her education that early. My grandma's mother suggested that they keep her periods a secret, and have my grandma continue school. She did. She would not attend school whenever she had her periods - they believed a menstruating woman was impure and had to be quarantined; despite their progressive stance on her education, her parents couldn't bring themselves to break this taboo – but she continued school until she graduated tenth grade.

Two of my mother's three sisters didn't go to college. None of her sisters had a proper career. Amidst all these women in my family, who had great potential but indelible societal boundaries limiting them, there was my aunt Sundari, my father's brother's wife. Aunt Sundari was the only woman I knew, as I was growing up, that had a job even though she didn't have to. Not just a job, a career that she enjoyed. Aunt Sundari is a big reason for my resolve to have a career and my pursuit of economic independence.

Aunt Sundari lived in Delhi with her husband and their son. Every time she visited us in Chennai, we would have memorably long conversations. A lot of these conversations were my rants, but many yielded wisdom that I would cherish to this day.

One day, as Aunt Sundari and I were leaning over the parapet of our open terrace, letting the salty air from the Bay of Bengal cool us, we talked about her job. I wanted to know all about working, as a woman. I had heard stories about my aunt's miserable commute in Delhi. She had to travel in a public bus, with men and women packed like the pulp of a grapefruit. She almost never found a seat and had to stand for the entire length of her journey. "Is it tough?" I asked her. Didn't she feel tired at the end of the day, coming home and still having to cook dinner for her family? Was it frightening to work with so many men around her?

Peppered with questions, Aunt Sundari looked at me for a long minute and nodded.

"Yes, it is tough," she said with pursed lips.

"Then why do you work?" I asked.

"Because Raji," she said, with a serious look on her face, "when you want to buy something as simple as a tube of lipstick, you should not have to stand in front of your husband for permission or money."

It took a bit of time for me to register what she had just said. But then I felt like a little candleflame was lit inside my head. Aunt Sundari worked because her work gave her freedom. It asserted her standing within her family. It allowed her to buy things for herself, without the need for anyone else's approval. It made her feel empowered. It may have been the precise moment that I became determined to find a profession and pursue a career. If I ever wanted to buy a tube of red lipstick, frivolous as it might be, I wanted the wherewithal to buy it. Not just a candleflame, but a fire was lit inside me.

Long after that, I would see many women around me treating their careers as optional, just as my cousin in Toronto was doing. I do believe that everyone should make their own choice on how they want to live their lives. Being a homemaker and caring for children is perfectly important – if unpaid – work. But an individual should have the freedom to make that choice intentionally and after considering the long-term consequences. Every time I see a woman choose to lean out either because the corporate norms do not work for her or because there is no equal partnership at home or because she is not self-confident, it pains me. I worry she has not thought it through, that she is putting the burden of her upkeep on someone else that might fail her. This person that she is relying on to support her for the rest of her life might disappear from her life or lose the ability to be gainfully employed.

Work - a career - is more than just a way to make a living. Work can make you confident in yourself. It can open new horizons, new experiences, new worldviews that might have been previously inaccessible. Work can give you purpose. It can help you develop new meaningful social connections. It can fill you with joy as you contribute to the success of others and feel proud of your own accomplishments. A mom with a career inspires her daughter to have a career of her own too; the daughter sees proof that it can be done. But more than anything, work can bring meaning to your life, social interactions that widen your horizon, richer experiences, and personal growth. Even if you had no financial reason to work, there is value that work brings on its own that makes a career worth going after.

Women in the past were barred from higher education or not allowed in the workplace. Over time, through many struggles, we won the right to work and earn our financial freedom. With every generation that passed, we became more educated, more powerful at the workplace. We still have ways to go toward equality at home and at work. The pandemic of 2020 has threatened to undo some of the gains we got in the workplace. Let's not throw away our hard-earned right to earn our financial freedom lightly. Let us strive for economic power. Let us stop seeing our careers as optional and flippant. Let's choose to be self-reliant. Let's get equipped with the skills, the knowledge, and the mindset to sustain ourselves.

Some parting thoughts

Do not lean out and stop working because you feel your career is optional. Work brings more value to you than just a paycheck.

You deserve to have a career and to stand on your own two legs.

If you must buy a tube of lipstick (or something considered needless in your world), you should not have to explain it to anyone. You should have the wherewithal to go get it on your own.

4

A path littered with rocks

My journey into tech

Sometime in 2019, there was a meme that got the Internet shimmering with energy. It was the "How it started" and "How it's going" meme. People posted pictures on social media that told the story of their relationship journeys, their weight loss journeys, and their addiction journeys.

If I were to post pictures of my career journey, the "How it started" would show me as a teenager at my friend's house using her computer because I couldn't afford one at mine. On the "How it's going" side, I'd have a collage of me coding at my desk at work, speaking in front of an audience, writing in my notebook, being with my team, running with my friends, and traveling with my husband. Today, these are all parts of my identity. I am a developer, a leader at a large technology company, a writer, a speaker, and a runner. I love traveling and mentoring people. But none of these were in my plans as a teenage girl. As a teenager, all I wanted to do when I grew up was to become a doctor.

A lot of kids growing up around the world would have said the same thing too. In India, in those days (and imaginably even today), there were just a few admired professions, and medicine was at the top. Perhaps this was partially why I wanted to become a doctor. I was a people-pleaser, a box-checker after all, and I wanted to check a box by achieving something on top of many people's lists. And I wanted to become a doctor because I wanted to be financially independent. But to be honest, it was a bit more than that. I wanted to solve important problems. I wanted to cure deadly diseases. I wanted to save people's lives. I wanted to be distinguished. In fact, so distinguished that I would get the Nobel prize in medicine. Alexander Fleming, the inventor of Penicillin, was one of my idols. I wanted to be him.

It was my dearest wish to become a doctor and a scientist that cured diseases. I spent many a lazy Indian afternoon, seated by our window covered with a mosquito net and specks of dust, daydreaming of the day when they would read out my name for the Nobel prize. My father supported and encouraged me in this. So, I diligently memorized diagrams from my biology textbooks. Cross-section of frogs and cockroaches, anatomy of lungs and the inner ear, stages of mitosis. My biology teacher, Ms. Hilda Jacintha, loved me. She thought I was sharp and studious. Despite my general disinclination toward art, I could draw anything in her class accurately.

But becoming a doctor was just not in the cards for me...

After my high school exams were done, I waited anxiously for my scores to be released. On the day that results came out, my dad and I went to my school together to get mine. I was shifting my weight from one leg to the other, restlessly kicking up the sand under my flip-flops, when my name was called out. The person at the counter asked my dad a few questions and handed us my mark sheet.

I looked at my scores and my heart sank. They were just not enough. Getting into medical college in India was no easy business. Not then, not now. Being born into one of the privileged castes meant I had a very small margin of error with my test scores if I wanted to get in. And I had failed to get in.

It was one of the saddest days of my life, and it was followed by more sad days. I was disappointed with myself. Many people tried to console me. My dad said that it was ok that I didn't get what I wanted. The universe had created a blank page for me, he said. I had to figure out how to fill it. A few days passed. I started coming out of my funk and talking to people – well-wishers, relatives, mentors, and friends. Many of them directed me to

Computer Science. Computers were all about solving problems, they said. "You like solving problems, and you are good at it. So why don't you give it a try?".

Thousands of miles away, almost around the same time, the technology sector was starting to boom. The Internet was becoming ubiquitous. Netscape's browser would soon become available to the public. Hotmail, one of the first web email services, was getting ready to be launched. Tech was beginning to show promise to change the world. I was intrigued.

I decided to study Computer Science.

You could say that I chanced upon technology, that I am an accidental techie. But ever since the day that I decided to become a programmer, my journey has been one of learning. The first years in college were hard. I noticed that my peers in college were way ahead of me. In coding labs, I was clumsy. I remember many anxious moments before our programming exams, when I'd sit on the staircase outside my college's Computer Science lab, memorizing the solutions in my textbook, line by line. Those exams filled me with terror, and my only goal was to somehow pass. Coming from a background of studying frogs and lungs, coding was too abstract. What were these bits and bytes my teacher was talking about? What did they look like inside a computer? Did they have shape or texture? Clearly, I had a steep learning curve ahead of me. I just couldn't wrap my head around the important, fundamental concepts. I felt I had made the wrong choice.

But I plodded on. By this point in my life, perseverance had become second nature. I memorized more, screwed up more, learned from the screw ups, and on repeat. Some day – I kept reminding myself - once I had mastered walking a tree depth-first and coding the Towers of Hanoi, I would solve real problems for real people.

As I was preparing to graduate from my undergrad school, the next big swerve in my life happened. I decided to get married to someone that my father had introduced me to just weeks before.

In India, deciding to marry someone can feel as whirlwind as a trip to a local *chaat* shop. While marriages last long – the couple typically works hard to make their marriage work, and the woman often cedes much ground in the process – wedding bells can toll quickly. My wedding bells certainly did.

After getting married, I moved in with my in-laws. My husband was a stranger at first. Someone I had worked hard to know better. But he was also kind and loving. Most importantly, he was different. He had unique ideas and was a feminist at heart. I could see right away that our relationship would work, that he would treat me as an equal. My love for him started to blossom.

In 1999, I moved to Canada with my new husband.

In our early days in Canada, I spent most of my afternoons at home alone. I was scared like a puppy in a new home, feeling lonely and small in a strange country thousands of miles from everything familiar. If the phone rang in those days, I did not have the courage to pick it up. I was too nervous to talk to anyone other than my husband. I didn't know if I would be able to understand or speak to the person on the other end. I avoided social engagements, especially with people that didn't speak my language. I didn't dare apply for a job. My undergrad education, where I had done enough to pass but not really understand much, gave me no confidence. I knew I needed to learn programming properly. I also needed to become fluent in English. I spent most of my childhood in mediocre schools in small towns. While I had learned to read and write English, I didn't speak it. Not fluently, at least.

In my isolation and boredom, I cast about for things to do. I borrowed stacks of books from the local library. I tried new recipes at home. One chilly afternoon, I laced up my sneakers and went for a run. I had never been physically active before, but I was getting desperate to keep myself occupied. Running seemed like a solitary activity that could give me comfort. As I headed out of my house, there was a light wind. The cherry blossom trees along my route were in full bloom. The air was crisp. I started jogging at a good clip. I felt free - free of my broken childhood, of my feelings of inadequacy in my field, of my limitations. My spirits lifted. I could do this forever, I thought. I kept running, and running, and running. I thought I must have run at least two miles, and that was when I felt a stabbing pain in my diaphragm. I had no more breath left in my lungs. I made a fist with my right hand and pressed it under my ribs. It felt as though my insides had been thrown into a sugarcane juicer. I gasped and bent forward. I turned to see how far I had come. I had run a block.

It was disappointing. I realized I was no natural runner – just like I was no natural programmer - but I wanted to go running again the next day. My endurance increased, day by day. I could run a block, then two, then a mile. My focus, my motivation, and my resolve felt strengthened. I applied to two universities in British Columbia, to their Computer Science Master's programs, and got into both. I enrolled in University of British Columbia.

After my two years of graduate School in Canada, However, I was still not a "finished product".

As soon as I finished grad school, I started looking for a job in tech. I interviewed at a company called Business Objects and failed my in-person interview. I interviewed at Amazon and failed my phone interview, even before I could see anyone in person. Rejections started piling up in my inbox. I was heartbroken, but I learned to nurse my feelings and forge ahead. In 2005, I interviewed at Microsoft. Finally, I got my break. I got an offer for an entry level job.

I joined Microsoft in November 2005. My new colleagues were brilliant, many of them nice, awkward, and quiet. I felt completely out of my depth beside them. There was a moment, during one of those dark winter nights in the Pacific Northwest, as I was walking from my office to my car in the parking lot, when I broke down crying. No one could see me; it was pitch dark. Hot tears kept rolling down my cheeks. Was I good enough for this job? Was I smart enough for these folks? These questions kept cascading inside my head. But I went home, and I consoled myself. As I lay in bed that night, going over my situation in my mind, I knew what I had to do. I had to focus on what I could learn and how I could make progress. I had to learn how to develop good code, to architect complex systems, to review other people's work, to test thoroughly, to persuade people of my ideas, and so much more.

I started learning from my work and from the people around me. I worked hard. I put in a lot of hours, sometimes staying up till two in the morning, debugging or learning something new or wrestling with some code. I made use of every piece of relevant feedback that I got. I gradually became a good developer and then an excellent developer on my team. Then I was asked to lead a team of developers. None of it, though, came easy.

I tell you of all my struggles in my journey in tech for three reasons. Firstly, I want you to know that you will feel uncomfortable in this journey and that's ok. Many of us have been there, in the trenches, and survived. Secondly, you never stop being a student. To this day, I am learning. There is always something to improve on, something to master. So, if you are feeling unworthy or deficient, know that other people around you are feeling it too. And lastly, your fears and anxieties never fully leave you. Years have passed since my early days in North America. In 2018, I keynoted at an auditorium filled with twenty thousand people. I talked about the software that my team was building. In the green room, as I was getting mic-ed up, those early days of my journey flashed through my head. It was a different me back then, but in some ways, still the same. A few aspects had changed - my comfort with English and my confidence in my professional skills had grown tremendously. But I still felt sorely inadequate in many areas. I was still gripped with dread as I waited in that green room. I am not fearless now that I am a seasoned professional - you never become fearless in this work. You just need to learn how to manage your fears.

As a girl, I wanted to become a doctor so I could touch people's lives with my work. I failed and pivoted to a technology career. Am I happy now that I made that switch? Heck, yes. Despite all the challenges and the inequities, being in tech, building things that can be used by millions if not a billion people, my work has been intensely meaningful. I love what I do, and I learn every day. Over time, I have become financially independent too. At Microsoft, we often talk about our mission to empower every person on the planet to achieve more. With tech, we can certainly do that.

Some parting thoughts

It's ok if your path is littered with rocks and stones. You will find a way through them.

Rejections do not portend permanent misery. They will pass and you will see success again.

Always be open to learning. Learning from others, learning from your failures, learning from your rejections.

Failures can fuel success. Do not give into despair.

You cannot foretell where your life will lead you. Follow your curiosity and connect the dots looking back.

II

Part Two

Professional Advice

5

The audacity within you

The case for being bold in your career

There is a fragment of memory in my head from when I was six years old that I go back to now and then.

I had just started first grade in a new school in Chennai and I hated it. Not liking your school is not an uncommon thing in kids, but I had extra dislike for my new school. After losing my mother, I had been yanked out of my school in the countryside and brought to the city. I missed my old friends, I missed my mom, and I was an utter misfit in the city school. Every minute I was in class, I was plotting to get out of there.

Then one fine day, I made it happen. It was about two in the afternoon. We had finished lunch and were going over English lessons. I went up to my teacher and told her I was not feeling well. My stomach hurt badly, and I wanted to go home. I told her I knew how to get to my grandparents' flat, and I would go there and rest up until my father came to get me. She knew that my grandparents lived nearby. She gave me permission to go, and I left. I found my way to my grandparents' flat.

Upon arriving there, grandma let me in, asked me to wash myself, and gave me a snack. I was enjoying being pampered in familiar surroundings when I heard a loud rap on the door. It was around four or five in the evening.

Grandma opened the door, and my dad burst in looking hot and angry. He rushed into the room where I was sitting, dragged me out, out of the house, down the staircase, through the courtyard where boys were playing cricket, and into an autorickshaw parked outside. He looked into my eyes, and sternly said, "Never ever do that again!" Clearly, he had been frantic about my whereabouts. Emotions poured through me. I felt chastised. I was suddenly afraid.

Many things about this incident and the memory of it elude me. For example: How did my teacher let me leave the school alone? Being new in the city, how did I know the way to my grandma's flat? How did a little girl walking alone escape the notice of the many vile elements in the city? Such is the nature of childhood memories: you wrestle with the fragments you can recall and stitch the hazy snapshots into a cogent narrative with many details missing.

But I tell you this story not just because I find it a notable episode in my life, albeit the missing details, but because there is some meaning in it that I feel is worth exploring.

It was the first time in my life that I remember being brave and going after what I wanted with confidence.

LET'S FAST FORWARD FIFTEEN YEARS.

I was a graduate student in the University of British Columbia. I had become increasingly drawn to the field of Distributed Systems. It was a hot subject of the day. I had taken a class from the professor that taught Distributed Systems in the university, and I longed to do my thesis in it. However, when the moment came, I grew afraid. I thought and thought and thought, and I began to feel that the subject was beyond me. Everyone I knew in the Distributed Systems lab was way smarter than me. I told myself I would likely not be successful in the field.

Doing my research in Distributed Systems would give me terrific learning, but it also presented a huge chance of failure. Doing research in Software Engineering or Databases, on the other hand, would be more up my alley and guaranteed better success. Or so I thought. I ended up choosing what I felt was the safer path. I did my thesis in Software Engineering.

I have often reflected, after my graduation, why I stopped myself from doing research in Distributed Systems. Why I felt I was not qualified or smart enough to succeed in the field. I never approached the professor to talk more about research in the subject. I didn't interview students in the lab to learn from their experience. I didn't go to the library, or use the Internet, to truly understand how difficult it might be. I just assumed that the subject was beyond me.

That turned out to be simply not true. I have done a lot of work now, since I made that decision, in Distributed Systems. I have built massive online services and complex client-server systems. With the benefit of hindsight, I've realized that my analysis of my own fitness for Distributed Systems research all those years ago was wrong. It was an irrational fear that I had allowed to take root in my heart and thereby miss an opportunity to do interesting work under a professor I respected.

FAST FORWARD ANOTHER FEW YEARS.

I was at Microsoft. At Microsoft, I learned many things: I learned the pride of craftsmanship, the satisfaction of making a difference, the value of diverse experiences and perspectives, the joy of making complex things happen, and what true leadership was all about. But there is one particular lesson from an old mentor that has been life changing. "Raji," he told me one day, "you are a good developer. People like working with you. You are persistent when you go after something. But there is one thing that is going to come in your way sooner or later."

I looked at him quizzically.

He continued. "You need to put yourself more out there. You need to take more risks, not just opt for safe, known things. That's how you can get to the more senior levels in this company."

I knew what he said was true. I had let my life experiences knock my natural audacity out of me. I had started playing to not lose, and instead I needed to play to win. This was no good. I started working on becoming more and more comfortable with risks since that conversation with him.

I started raising my hand for projects that were going badly so I could help turn them around. I said yes to speaking in public more. I set my eyes on startup opportunities that had big potential for success but also a chance of things falling apart. I began to challenge the negative self-talk we all develop over years of growing up and trying to please society.

I have learned through these years that there are no two ways about it...

To become truly who you can be, to become excellent at your work, you need to be audacious. You need to be willing to stick your neck out now and then.

The six-year-old girl that left her school that day showed audacity. She found what her heart desired and boldly went after it. No one taught her how to do it, nor inspired her to do it, she just did it. Granted many things could have gone wrong that day. And I am not by any means advocating letting schoolchildren roam freely in the streets - that indeed would be an irresponsible thing to do. But my point is that courage is innate to us. As children, we constantly push the envelope of possibilities in front of us. We don't overthink the failure case. Our goal is rarely to impress anyone or to show people how bold or smart or successful we are. We do things for the joy of doing them. We run around just to feel the rush of air through our hair, climb trees or jungle gyms, do things most adults would consider insane. We know how to feel alive and how to experiment. It's not that we don't fear the unknown - we are afraid of the dark, for example - but we are curious, we learn constantly, and we want to try things out for ourselves.

Over time we become more interested in playing safe. We overestimate our chances of failure and stop ourselves from doing things we truly want to do. We learn to become more afraid of risks. Paradoxically, we become less confident in ourselves. We crave approval and 'not looking bad'.

While it is only wise to carefully evaluate our desires and actions, let's stop overdoing it. Our goal should be the pinnacle of who we individually can be. To reach that, we need to show the audacity that we once showed as children. Let's challenge the inner voice that takes us away from it. Let's not become imprisoned within the walls of our fears. For as Theodore Roosevelt said:

"It is hard to fail, but it is worse never to have tried to succeed." — Theodore Roosevelt

Some parting thoughts

Be audacious. Take some risks with the projects you sign up for.

Do not overthink the failure case. Know that the skies won't fall if you hit obstacles, or your effort fails.

6

Make friends with fear

How to deal with fear of the unknown

When I left India for good in 1999, I left my family behind. I left my familiar culture behind. I had no clue how to make friends in my new world, how to get a job, how to live happily and fruitfully. On the day I said goodbye to my folks – my father kissing me on my forehead, my mother-in-law holding my moist hand – I was not sure how my life would turn out after I made my journey. It is every young person's rite of passage to peek into this dark door of the future that is unknown. For an immigrant young person though, moving to a strange land that she had never lived in before, the fear can be doubly intense. My heart was racing, partly from excitement and partly from nervousness.

I would experience that feeling – that part excitement, part nervousness – over and over in my career. Every time I have raised my hand to do something that was beyond what I had done before, I have felt it. Every time I've walked into a meeting room full of very senior people, I have felt it. Every time I've stood in front of a group of people to give a talk, I have felt it. And, on the personal side, every time I decided to climb a rockier mountain, run a longer distance, or write a potentially unpopular article, I have felt it.

Let me tell you of the time my husband and I decided to cycle along the pacific coast, covering about nine hundred miles from Vancouver, British Columbia to Brookings, Oregon in three weeks. We packed all that we needed for those three weeks in our pannier bags, hitched to our bikes. We carried a tent, a stove, some fuel, and some backpacking food we could cook in our campsite every night. Now, I had never properly learned bicycling. Growing up, my grandma had frowned upon women who bicycled. It could lead to dissipation and dissolution, she had declared. Still, after a lot of hot arguing, she assented. She hired someone to teach me the basics, and I learned how to go from one point to another, in a straight line, on my brother's bike. I learned to stay upright and not fall. I learned to make forward progress, and then brake and dismount when needed. But I didn't know how to turn, how to take my hand off the handlebar while pedaling, or how to pedal up a hill standing up. I would learn some of these skills later in my life, in the quiet, leafy streets of Vancouver where I attended grad school, but I had never been very comfortable on my bike.

So, naturally, when we discussed the idea of biking down the pacific coast for three weeks, I was filled with trepidation. Would I be able to do it? Would I crash? What happens if I got into an accident because I couldn't balance on my bike? Fears animated my mind. But I also knew that it would be a remarkable, once-in-a-lifetime experience. I closed my eyes and told myself that I would go for it. I had my husband with me, and we pledged to start slow. I promised to train before we started the trip, by commuting every day to work. I would practice with loaded panniers on the bike, practice switching gears, pedaling a considerable number of miles, and just being comfortable on my bike. When we started our tour, we would take it slow, and I would slowly gain confidence. This was our plan.

And our plan worked. Despite my fears and worries, I was fine. My husband and I pedaled down the pacific coast, all the way to the Oregon-California border, that summer. It was hard work, but it was also a splendid trip. Highway 101 is a pretty road that goes up and down the coast, taking us along thickly wooded forests and a sparkling blue ocean. We slept beneath the dark blanket of a sky dotted with stars, listening to waves lapping in and out of the shore. We visited small towns with just a few shacks and a church, and big cities with restaurants serving organic, vegan ice cream. I grew closer to my husband, he and I now supporting each other for - literally - our dear lives. It was one of my most memorable trips, and I could only have had that experience because I said no to my fears.

Let's talk about another time I did the same – subdued my fears so I could do big, interesting things - this time, at work. In 2018, as an Engineering Manager at Microsoft, I was on a business trip to London. I was sitting in the hotel lobby, when I struck up a conversation with a man whom we shall call Brett. Brett was also from Microsoft. His job at the company was to organize demos and speeches for big conferences. I told him that I was interested in public speaking myself and was in fact in London, at that moment, to keynote at an event.

To be honest, I was not – and still am not - a natural at public speaking. I have worked hard for every single talk I have delivered. I have always felt intimidated by even the idea of an audience of more than ten people. But I knew it was important to communicate to big groups of people as I grew in my career. So, I had been on the lookout for opportunities to practice the skill.

As Brett and I got to know each other more, he made a proposal. He was looking for speakers for an upcoming conference called Microsoft Inspire, and he asked if I could do the demos at the keynote of that event. I was jolted into alertness as he said that. Microsoft Inspire was routinely attended by over ten thousand people in big sports arenas. A keynote is the central event of the conference, with an enormous stage. Until then, my biggest audience had been three hundred people. I didn't have the slightest clue how to talk to such a big crowd. Of course, fear started to spread inside me like exhaust from a pipe as soon as I started contemplating what I had to do. But I said yes to Brett. This was a big, exciting chance. Few people get to present in an arena with that many people, and I would learn a lot from the experience. I was not a hundred percent qualified or prepared for it at that moment, but I knew I would learn.

The run-up to the event involved a lot of hard work. I practiced in front of my mirror, I practiced in front of my husband, I taped myself and watched it, and I rehearsed with my demo team. I got a ton of feedback and got better with every rehearsal. On the day of the event, as I sipped hot tea in an overly air-conditioned green room, I felt both hot and cold. I felt the infamous butterflies in my stomach. My heart was thudding to the clip of some upbeat music in a club. But as I waited there, counting the minutes before I went on stage, I did a few things that helped me.

I recognized and acknowledged my fear. The first step to dealing with an issue is to acknowledge it. I took a deep breath and observed how my fear was coursing through my system. I felt heat rise in my chest, and energy bubble furiously into my hands. My breath was shallow. These were my fear symptoms. I recognized them and admitted to myself that "I was feeling fear".

I reminded myself I'd not get out the door if I anchored on everything that could go wrong. It may be a dangerous business going out your front door, but you cannot live sheltered in a dungeon forever. That is not how life is meant to be lived. I reminded myself of this perspective and assumed a more optimistic outlook. Most likely, after all that practice that I had done, I was going to do fine.

I harked back to all the times that I survived what I thought was impossible. I thought back to the time when I summited peaks that I thought were beyond my abilities. I thought back to the time I had successfully cycled down the pacific coast. I had it in me, I knew, to do the things that I set my mind to.

I reframed my fear. I told myself what I was feeling was not nervousness, but excitement. That was true anyway, I was excited to go out to an arena filled with people. I wanted to find out what it felt like to talk to a crowd of that size. The people there were not assembled to heckle and boo me, they were there to learn from what I had to say. In fact, they wanted me to succeed. These were *my* people, so there was no need to be intimidated by them.

When I finally went on the stage, I heard applause from the crowd. I felt the energy throbbing like a physical thing in the stadium. I spoke the words I had rehearsed. I smiled, thanked the audience, and left. It went fine after all, just like the other hundred times I have done something completely frightening.

Ancient explorers are often touted as brave. I don't think they lacked fear. Fear is an essential emotion – it is an evolutionary instinct to point us to immediate danger. But fear can become limiting when not properly dealt with. Ancient explorers were not fearless, they were masters at dealing with fear.

I feel discomfort and fear every time I stare at an unknown situation. But I deal with it. Little by little, one can travel far. I remind myself that I can always take a little step forward.

Here are some things to try

The next time you are facing a daunting task, do the following:

Recognize your symptoms of fear and acknowledge them.

Take on an optimistic outlook. Tell yourself things will go fine, and you will never venture out the door if you thought everything you did could fail in some way.

Think of the times you have done big things that you felt were beyond your comfort zone. Let these times boost your self-confidence.

Reframe your fear as excitement and anticipation.

Some parting thoughts

Embrace the unknown and raise your hand for bold, epic opportunities in your career. You will do fine, and you will learn things from the experience. More than anything, you will improve your self-confidence by doing things that you once thought were impossible for you.

7

Be a changeling

Why you should reinvent yourself often

When I started at Microsoft, I had been trained for six years in Computer Science. I came into the company as a coder. My identity was tied up around coding, and I worked hard to become good at it. In my early years at the company, I was working in a programming language called C#. Slowly, I learned other technologies that were in use in my team. I started working in a relational database query language called SQL. I learned to write scripts and use Microsoft's internal tools and frameworks.

But the field of tech is ever-changing. I could not master one thing and just rest on my laurels for the next decade. I had to keep running to keep up. In a way, I love that about being in tech. You are never quite done being a student. You are always learning new concepts, new paradigms, new languages, and new technologies. It is quite exhilarating. In my career, relational databases gave way to NoSQL databases that stored massive amounts of data. New ways of thinking were constantly emerging. I had been immersed in Object-Oriented Programming when I started. When Functional Programming came on the scene, I enthusiastically embraced it. Big Data was starting to change the world, and I embraced that too. Every change required that I unlearn a few things I had taken for granted and learn other things.

It was not just technologies that I had to keep up with. I had to learn to rapidly reinvent myself every so often. A few years into my life as a coder, I began to see a shift in the work I was gravitating toward. I was a senior member of the team, and now a lot of my time was spent reviewing other people's work. I was slowly becoming an architect in the team. Then I was asked to lead a team of engineers and I said yes to that. I became a manager, and I had to learn what people management and leadership meant. My energies were now being channeled increasingly into learning people skills. As I learned my ropes there, my identity was still getting morphed as the situation demanded. I became a mentor for newcomers and an interviewer for the company.

In the summer of 2017, I went on a recruiting trip to my alma mater, University of British Columbia. During the trip, I was disappointed by the lack of diversity in the pipeline. I became more disappointed when the few diverse candidates that were in our interview loops didn't make it through. When I returned, I wanted to do something about it. I started pitching – to anyone that wanted to hear – the idea of running bootcamps to help diverse candidates in universities get ready for interviews in software companies. My plan was to find organizations catering to diverse students in universities and work with them to train students on interviewing at large tech companies. This, I believed, would give a boost of confidence to these underrepresented students, students that seemed to be displaying a lack of confidence, much more so than their counterparts.

My idea didn't gain much traction within the company. *C'est la vie.* It happens to the best of us - not everything that we want to do will become a reality. But soon, dots began to connect in other ways. Unbeknownst to me, at that exact moment, there was a virtual team being formed in my organization to run a bootcamp in in Lagos, Nigeria for entrepreneurs that were starting businesses for social good in their own communities.

The word bootcamp must have triggered a connection. I was asked if I wanted to be on that team. This opportunity was certainly out of left field for me. I had never worked with startups or entrepreneurs before. I had never been a coach or public speaker outside my small team. But I knew that this could give me great learning. It would also be a chance for me to help others, which is exactly what I had wanted to do when I had pitched the bootcamp idea earlier. It sounded perfect. I raised my hand.

Being a mentor to African entrepreneurs ended up being one of the richest experiences I have had in my career. But it also asked more of me than what I had at the time. I had to morph myself from being a coder and a manager into being a coach, a speaker, and one with a mind for business. I applied myself to learning all of that. I nervously gave my first talks to the entrepreneurs that we were coaching. I worked with someone on the team who had an MBA to learn how to review Profit and Loss and Cash Flow statements. I listened to others who taught these entrepreneurs about business models, customer canvasses, and Minimum Viable Products and absorbed all that information like a potato dropped in a cauldron of soup absorbs flavors. Soon I started taking on other identities at work. I was now a public speaker, a coach, and someone who knew how to build startups.

These new dimensions would become essential parts of my career soon. I was beginning to get invited to give talks outside work, which was particularly helpful as I started leading bigger teams at work. My managers started trusting me with building startups within Microsoft, taking ideas from scrawls on a napkin to successful products used by millions of people. Of course, I didn't go after any of these opportunities intentionally. But when they came to my doorstep, I invited them in for tea. I was open to reinventing myself. I raised my hand. I was open to being a changeling, to stretching my range of capabilities.

But how do you stretch your range if you do not currently see any opportunity to do so at work? What if, at your workplace, you are required to just do your primary job and nothing else? One way is to develop interests outside of work. Dona Sarkar, a Program Manager at Microsoft, puts it memorably. She says that, since she was not born a cat that could 'live nine lives', she decided to live nine lives in one. She is a fashion designer, public speaker, blogger, an author of fiction and non-fiction books, an artist, and so much more. She has actively created these other venues for her creativity, her curiosity, and her productivity. She has forged her identity out of many things, leery of putting all her "emotional eggs into one basket" – her day job.

There is good scientific reasoning for developing such varied interests and the advantage that it can offer you in your career. Psychologists warn us against the rigidity you can develop in your brain if you become too entrenched in just one domain. They call it *cognitive entrenchment*. Eric Dane, a Rice University professor, exhorts people to step outside their domain to develop mental agility.

Many scientists and Nobel Prize winners do this admirably. They have hobbies that they devote themselves to outside their work. They are poets, writers, sculptors, welders, woodworkers, photographers, and musicians. I know many successful people in tech, of all genders, that have such varied interests too. One of my colleagues, a Corporate Vice President, is an Amateur Radio enthusiast. He fiddles with frequencies and transceivers to communicate with fellow hobbyists.

Another colleague is a video blogger who talks about coding on Tik Tok and YouTube. A friend, who is an outstanding Software Architect, is also a part-time chef. Laura Butler, who was the first female Technical Fellow at Microsoft, once took a yearlong break from her career to travel, learn acrobatics, do improv comedy, and run marathons. While you may not be in a position in your life to take such extended breaks, you can try to find a few hours on your weekends and evenings to pursue an interest outside of your domain.

In his famous commencement speech, Steve Jobs told us to collect our dots first. You may not know how these dots will connect in the future, he said, but they will. He never thought his interest in calligraphy, while he was in college, would lead to anything productive. But it did. It helped him design fabulous fonts for the Macintosh computer.

So, my advice to you is this: Raise your hand for interesting opportunities that surprise you and leave you wondering if you have what it takes to do well on them. Be ok with being a changeling, a magus who can shift identities when called for. Specializing in one thing is great, but in fields as versatile and human-centric as tech, you will have more success being someone who can don many hats and speak many languages.

Some parting thoughts

When opportunities knock on your door, invite them in.

Embrace change.

Be open to reinventing yourself.

In tech, being a generalist and being able to do many things with comfort can be an advantage.

8

The Jitterbug

How to deal with meeting jitters and get your voice heard

You are in a meeting and you really, really, want to say something. Suddenly you feel your stomach curdle. Your heart beats fast. Your face flushes, and your throat dries up. You freeze, and you just can't get your words out. This happens when you are about to deliver a talk to an audience as well. I am frequently asked how to overcome this panic. What are some ways in which one can contribute something meaningful in such discussions in a way that lands well with the audience?

FIRST OFF, I GET YOU. I TRULY, WHOLE-HEARTEDLY GET YOU.

I am an introvert at heart. I shy away from speaking in front of many people too. I have avoided my share of big parties in my life, and I have felt the terror of losing fluency.

But I have also realized that getting better at communicating to groups of people is not just a skill that will help you excel at your job, but in careers like software building, it is almost table stakes. Software building is a team sport, and you get bigger things accomplished by influencing, sharing, and engaging with other people. So yes, despite not being in your comfort zone, it is something you WILL want to get good at.

LET'S START WITH WHY YOU MIGHT FEEL THE WAY YOU FEEL WHEN

SPEAKING IN A MEETING

When you finish reading this chapter, do this. Take a blank sheet of paper. Find yourself some quiet time and a cozy spot to do some reflection. Think: what causes you to feel anxious when you are speaking in a meeting?

Here is a list of reasons I have discovered in myself and heard from others, with some antidotes that might help.

You have a need to be liked and approved by others

Wanting to be liked is only too normal. Humans are social animals, and our ancestors' survival has very often depended on being liked by the people surrounding them. But then, it's ok to be not liked by 100% of your people 100% of the time. It's ok. Give yourself that permission. How others react to you, or your work, or what you're saying is not truly in your control, so stop trying too hard to influence an outcome. You should always have your audience's interests and worldview in mind, but that is not all there is to it. Do your best to appeal to your audience but remember you cannot control their reactions no matter how much you try.

You worry you don't know your material

Preparation and knowing your area do go a long way to making you comfortable. But you likely know your material more than most people in the audience. Being unsure of oneself is a quality that is more often found in folks coming from underprivileged backgrounds than ones that grew up with privilege. Privilege seems to instill confidence in people. Therefore, minorities in tech prepare for meetings way more than needed. I am not arguing for going into meetings completely unprepared, but I am arguing for balancing preparation with self-confidence and growth mindset.

Let's say you go into a meeting, and you don't know everything there is to it. What's the worst that can happen? You will learn something new from your colleagues, perhaps? It's not the end of the world. Approach the exercise with curiosity and an opportunity to learn something you didn't know before and it will calm your mind.

You think you are not eloquent, not funny, not charismatic, not XYZ

But you are you, and your perspectives are worthy of being heard. People in your meeting are generally there for some benefit to themselves: to learn something new, get something done, etc. Unless you are a stage performer or a stand-up comedian, they are not there to be inspired by your eloquence or humor or appearance. Even if you are on camera, there is no need to perform to the camera. Focus on your content, be you, and things will be ok.

You are a perfectionist, and you want to impress with perfection

In one of my favorite books, Pride and Prejudice, Elizabeth Bennet remarks to Mr. Darcy: "We are each of an unsocial, taciturn disposition, unwilling to speak, unless we expect to say something that will amaze the whole room". May be that is not EXACTLY you, but you still highly value creating a great impression. But do remind yourself that you're only human and it's ok to be less than perfect. In fact, go one step further and give yourself permission to be dull. Remind yourself that your purpose in speaking in that meeting is for the sake of giving something to your audience: educating them, offering a different point of view, bringing some issue to the forefront and so on. Or perhaps you want to speak to bring something back to your own team – for example, clarity, representation, feedback, or visibility. But the goal, most likely, is not for you to become the star of a performance. Unless you are an actor in a theater, you are not there to cement your stardom and wow everyone with your charisma and communication.

You think people are evaluating you for every mistake you make

Now, let's be real. People are generally caught up in their own worlds. The person they care about most is themselves. They are typically distracted, forgetful, and not that observant. Nine times out of ten, they are not looking for you to fail, in fact quite the opposite. And if they do notice something amiss, they are bound to forget it five days hence. The person that is likely to notice, remember, and not forgive any of your mistakes is...drum roll please...you. So, don't be hard on yourself. Remind yourself that people will be people, and not your personal Chitragupta or Saint Peter standing at the gates of heaven.

You sense doubt and translate that to danger

This is not surprising. Your brain is built to do exactly that, and you should use every bit of emotional intelligence to thwart it. You are uncertain of an unknown outcome. Why should you not be? No one can predict the future accurately. Your brain translates that uncertainty to a threat signal. Your limbic system - that part of our brains that we share with reptiles - gets engaged quickly and you display the typical "fight-or-flight" response.

To help pull myself out of such lizard-brained threat responses, I have a post-it note stuck on my desk. It says, "Be in the moment". That reminder helps bring my attention back to the present. I snap out of my anxieties and consciously listen to what's going on around me. I orient myself by noticing the objects in the room, labeling them inside my head, calling out their colors and names silently. I ground myself, feeling my feet on the floor, my back against the chair, my body being supported by the earth. I then find my center by breathing in deep and breathing out all the air in my lungs. Three times. These rituals help a ton in calming my nerves.

You anticipate and catastrophize every failure

A classic cognitive distortion. You evaluate your situation pessimistically and therefore think your efforts are certainly going to fail. But no one can predict the future, remember? Also, that nightmare of you living under the bridge, sans pennies and friends, just because you screwed up something at work, is likely just that. A figment of your imagination.

I've lived through some terrible things in my life, some of which actually happened.— Mark Twain

You attach too much importance to the people surrounding you at work/social life

As you reflect, imagine ten years from now. Do you see the people you so want to get the approval of in your life? I know, I know, I just said you can't predict the future. But the point is that most people in your work life and social life today are transient. There are very few people that you should really give two figs about. These are your keepers. The mentors you trust, the friends that make you better, the family that wants the best for you. Select them carefully. These are people you can attach all the importance to, but they are not waiting for the moment you fail.

Liberate yourself. If your anxiety comes from serious medical issues, seek help. Otherwise, when you feel that thudding heart, that sweat in your palms, take a moment to analyze the core of your emotion. Develop antidotes and deploy strategies like above to deal with them. Slow down, pause, and remember to take breaths as you speak. Don't be monotonous and try not to ramble. Rehearse if it's a big event and you are not up to winging it yet. Speak your audience's language. Smile, and have fun.

Here are some things to try

Next time before you go into a meeting, if you are feeling nervous, take some time to reflect on why you are feeling that way. Based on your reasons, think of strategies you can employ to calm your nerves. Write them down. Now take a few deep breaths and proceed into your meeting.

Some parting thoughts

You cannot control people's reactions to what you say. Do your best to land your perspectives well but do not concern yourself with being liked or approved.

Prepare, if you like, before meetings. But don't worry about being perfect. Think: what is the worst that can happen if you do not have answers to all the questions that come up? Most likely, it won't be catastrophic.

People around you at work today may not be around you ten years from now. It doesn't really matter what they think about you.

People do not come to work with the goal to notice every one of your screw-ups and judge you harshly. So, you can relax.

9

Slay the green-eyed demon

How to deal with dissatisfaction in your career that arises from comparisons

What is your first reaction when you hear that a friend or a colleague just got promoted? Do you instantly compare yourself to them? Do you feel an ugly sense of anger, shame, or disappointment with yourself?

This was the topic of one of my mentoring conversations. It was a stormy Friday evening in December. The wind outside was lashing my windows with rainwater. I was having a one-on-one meeting with a young woman that I mentor at work, whom we shall call Ashley. Ashley had just heard that her friend - someone she had graduated with from college - was getting promoted to the Principal level at her company. When she heard the news, Ashley mouthed words of congrats to her friend. Then she quickly turned a glaring white spotlight on herself. She felt bad about her own progress and wondered why she was not as successful as her friend.

As soon as she asked that question, she became suffused with unpleasant feelings. Her head clouded up, she lost interest in her work, and she even questioned if she belonged in this field at all. What began as a friendly conversation between her friend and her threatened to become a crisis in her career. But Ashley was keen enough to notice her tobogganing descent into this unhappy place. She realized she had to stop the slide and stop feeling bad. That's when she called me.

COMPARISONS AND ENVY COME UP A LOT IN MY CONVERSATIONS, NOT JUST WITH ASHLEY THAT DAY.

There are, of course, many nefarious reasons why some people - especially the ones that are quieter, that are minorities in tech - can get recognized less than others. But Ashley was not there to talk about these systemic issues in the industry. She was also not talking about her own ambitions. Ashley, instead, wanted to talk about her state of mind. How she was reacting to her friend's news and what she could do about it.

Let's start by looking at why we compare our lives with others. A lot of us in our industry have been schooled in competition and we revel in it. Our schools graded us on a curve. Only one boy or girl could hold the highest rank in class. Our teachers pinned little stars in our notebooks when we did well. We got little trinkets to celebrate our excellence. There could only be one winner in most sports, and that winner got all the glory. Slowly, this engineering shaped us.

Many of us have come to believe that external validation is what makes us worthy.

We have come to crave the adult version of those stars and trinkets: promotions, compliments, awards, and so on. We compare constantly. Is his child doing better than mine? Is she slimmer than me? Is he more liked? Social media fuels and stokes this burning unrest in our hearts and makes us ceaselessly unsure of ourselves.

Of course, I'm no stranger to this comparison habit. I grew up with a brother and many cousins, and I breathed comparison like it was oxygen. I wanted to sing better than my cousin, get better test scores than my brother, have prettier clothes than my friends. Later in my life too, I compared and benchmarked my life against others. But I have also come to realize that envy is generally an unworthy, harmful, unproductive, and irrational emotion.

Let's think: how does envy REALLY help? There are emotions that can rattle you into action. When you feel angry, for example, you might be railing against an injustice that needs to be corrected. Your anger can spur you to do that. Love could be a compass pointing to safety, comfort, and other good things in life. But envy? It generally makes you feel bad about yourself and makes your blood pressure rise. Your future actions get muddled and your hopes diminish. There are times when envy prompts you to evaluate your situation objectively and leave toxic ones, but more often than not, you are just paralyzed by the feeling.

SO HOW DO YOU DEAL WITH THIS FUTILE EMOTION?

Firstly, like Ashley did, become aware of what is going on inside you. Give yourself a time-out and go sit mindfully with your breath. Maybe for ten minutes, maybe for twenty. Breathe in, breathe out, and watch the emotion spread in your mind like a drop of black ink spilled on cream paper. Then reason over it. Tell yourself why the comparison doesn't make any sense. Your journey in life is distinct and different from anyone else's. Comparing your journey to others' is as absurd as comparing Jane Eyre's life with Lisbeth Salander's. There are things others have that you don't, and vice versa, and that is ok. Feeling envy won't magically lift you up or make your suffering disappear. In fact, quite the opposite.

Remind yourself that, regardless of what those stars and awards would have you believe, your value comes from within. You're a valuable person no matter your status, the number of cars you own, the number of pearls in your jewel box, or the number of followers you have on social media. You have talents and skills that you have developed over the years. You have battled hardships and won many victories against them. You do good work that makes you happy and proud. You try to be and ARE a good human. Affirm to yourself: "I am enough; strong enough, smart enough, eloquent enough, interesting enough, clever enough. I am enough." Finally, resolve to let the feeling go. But even after all this inner work, the tendency to compare can be a stubborn customer. Like me, you likely won't get it right 100% of the time, but you get better with practice.

I listened to Ashley and told her that she was not a bad person for feeling the way she was feeling. It is only human to feel, and feelings come packaged like snack boxes. There are snacks in the box that are good for you - like nuts -

and there are snacks you might do well to avoid - like hard candies and buttery cookies. The key is to distinguish them and attempt to subdue the ones that are destructive. Mindfulness, reasoning, self-affirmation, and letting go are steps that can help you with that.

When I ended the call with Ashley, the storm outside had abated and a surreal quiet had descended on the streets. I knew Ashley was already on the first step to mastering her emotions. She had become aware of what she was feeling and why that was bad. Now onward to the next steps. I wished her luck, and we said goodbye.

Some parting thoughts

Envy is a futile emotion. Learn to deal with it mindfully and rationally.

Your value doesn't come from external valuation or validation.

A lot of us constantly compare ourselves to others. This often comes from how we have been educated. The "star pupil syndrome" can hurt your emotional well-being and can affect your work, so it is best to stop being victim to it.

10

The stories we tell ourselves

How to stop telling yourself harmful stories

Recently, when I was out on one of my morning runs, I started thinking about mists. It was a fall morning, and the trail where I ran was whimsical, almost like I was on the movie set of the Lord of the Rings. The blades of grass by the trail shimmered with dew. The trees glowed red, red as apples. My breath, in out, in out, pooled in front of my face. I could hear the squelch of the leaves under my feet with every step. A mist had settled in the valley. Soft sunshine filtered through. The mist felt light on the skin and looked magical, but it also made things a little more uncertain. A little more dramatic.

Our minds have mists like that valley mist too. Neuropsychologists call them *Cognitive Distortions*. Buddhists call them the *Veils of Maya*. The Buddhist view is that we experience reality through Maya – a mist of perceptions and stories that we tell ourselves.

Telling stories to ourselves comes naturally to humans. As the author Joan Didion wrote, "We tell stories in order to live." Our ancestors certainly did that, in their uncertain and mostly unknown world:

"There is something dark and solid near the shrub. It could be a coyote."

"That thing on the ground looks like a snake. Don't step on it."

Even if ninety-nine times out of a hundred, it turned out to be just a tree stump (not a coyote) or just a coil of rope (not a snake), the one time that it was not, that story would have saved our ancestors.

These stories are our interpreted versions of what is happening around us, and what is happening to us. They help us understand what lies ahead and what course we should take. We perceive most of reality inside our heads, as stories. The world is constructed for us meticulously, by our minds, scene by scene. This construction is influenced by various signals: data streaming in through our senses, our memories, our hormones, cultural lessons we have learned, our emotions and so on. The mental stories are meant to represent reality...except when they do not. Many times, they turn out to be false: false alarms and false interpretations.

WE DON'T ALWAYS REMEMBER, HOWEVER, THAT OUR STORIES ARE JUST STORIES, AND CAN BE FALSE.

We react to them as though they are undeniable truths. Let me give you an example from my own life. A few years ago, when I had just started at Microsoft, I used to work with a guy whom we shall Jason. Jason was my then "archnemesis". He was the proverbial pain in my neck. On many occasions, he would tear apart my work in code reviews and design reviews. He frequently came across as rude/mean. I would seethe and fume, or feel belittled and humiliated, after many interactions with him.

Jason is no longer with Microsoft. That has nothing to do with me or his own attitude. He just no longer works here. But my point is, I made up so many stories about why Jason did what he did (he thought I was an idiot), what was going to happen to me because of him (I'd surely get fired thanks to his public evisceration of me), and what kind of a person Jason was (he was pure evil). I never actually spoke to him outright about any of this. I just made up stories in my head – convenient and habitual as such self-storytelling was.

In the two years Jason and I worked together, these stories caused me a lot of pain. Were they true? With the benefit of hindsight, I don't think so. Did they help me? Maybe a smidgen. I likely became more thorough thanks to the endless revising and cross-checking I did to avoid Jason's criticisms.

Overall, though, these stories hurt my mental health more than they helped my growth.

I was made to believe that things were more disastrous than they were, more personal than they were, more permanent than they were, and more pervasive than they were. My primordial danger-alert system that had evolved to pick up minute signals of potential threats (Snake! Coyote!) misfired and overreacted, creating more false alarms than actual signals.

My executive coach once told me that many of us climb what is known as the "ladder of inference". A ladder that describes our subliminal thinking process where we go from facts to selective reality to interpreted reality to assumptions to conclusions to beliefs to actions. I was climbing the ladder of inference, at quite a good clip, when I saw Jason send me critical feedback on my code and inferred that he was only ever sending me critical feedback. This led to my assumption that Jason didn't like me, which then led to my concluding that Jason is a bad person with prejudices, to the belief that I will get fired because of Jason. That made me anxious and defensive in my responses back to Jason. These are all stories that went on in my head as I climbed that ladder.

To keep my stories from directing me, to lift the veils of Maya in my mind, I had to put in a ton of actual work. This work has included everything from working with a coach, to routine journaling, to practicing mindfulness. To live peacefully and positively, you – like me - may need to step out of your stories and get a better grip on reality.

We tell ourselves stories that can cause pain, like the instance with Jason above, but also ones that can cause joy. We can delude ourselves about love, admiration, passion, and so on. In mindfulness, there is a four-step process to stop these stories from ruling over you. It is memorably called RAIN. When you're amid intense emotions, simply sit down somewhere quiet and close your eyes - or write in your journal - while following these steps.

1. **Recognize**: First, recognize you are playing a story in your head. This story may or may not be factual. In the case of Jason from my earlier experience, my first step would be to interrupt my seething and fuming and recognize that I am in the middle of an elaborate self-made movie.

2. **Allow**: Then, I should allow the story and the emotions it creates to exist

in my head. That may sound counter-intuitive, but have you ever tried to banish the thought of a big, fluffy panda bear by trying to forget about a big, fluffy panda bear? It's the same logic. I cannot deal with the story effectively by trying to forget about it. I should just observe my fears, my humiliations, and the helplessness in my head with some cognitive distance.

3. **Investigate**: Now I should look at the story from all angles. Hold it up to some mental light. Separate what appears to be facts from what appears to be layers of emotions surrounding the facts. Be curious about the shape of that story, and why it is thus. What caused me to come to the conclusions I came to about Jason? Can there be an alternate interpretation, no relation to me or my abilities? Can Jason just be pointing out the facts, in his own way?

4. **Non-Identify**: I know, non-identify is not an ACTUAL word. But the essence of this step is detaching from your mental stories. That is, in this case, I stop identifying myself with what I think Jason's behavior means about me. I should stop identifying reality with the story in my head about it.

While this is all nicely packaged as a memorable acronym, you really don't have to obsess over the detail of each of these steps. The key is simply to stop, observe, and detach from your emotions and stories. Do I get it right all the time? Definitely not. But I continue to practice and see progress.

Maya in Sanskrit means magic as well as illusions. Stories can indeed be magical. Cognitive illusions – false as they may be - evolved for a good reason. Mindfulness lets you separate the harmful illusions from the inspiring ones. It helps you become the master of your stories and keep your stories from becoming the master of you.

Here are some things to try

Are you feeling anxiety or worry about something going on at work? Try to get some cognitive distance from your stories by using the RAIN framework: Recognize, Allow, Investigate, Non-identify.

To learn more about mindfulness, check out the books I have recommended in the Resources chapter of this book.

Some parting thoughts

We tell ourselves too many stories every day. Some of these stories are helpful, but most harm us. They harm our mental peace, and our focused work.

Learn to deal with the stories in your head using mindfulness exercises.

11

It may be time to let go

How you move on from deadbeat projects and ideas

"What is the worst that can happen if you let go?" A dear friend asked me this question as I was agonizing over an important career decision. We were standing in line to pick up lunch at a hole-in-the-wall Indian eatery. It was a breezy summer afternoon, and mouthwatering aromas of curries filled the place.

I had just told her about a project that I had been working on for a few years. I had started working on the project with great enthusiasm. It had held much promise for the business and was terribly exciting. Over time though, it lost its luster. The business had moved on, and there were other more powerful opportunities to pursue. I had lost all passion for it. However, I did not stop working on it. Day after day, I endeavored. The more time I spent on the project, the more disinterested I became and the more miserable I felt. And yet, I held on.

Have you felt that way about a project you were working on? You know it has become deadbeat, and yet you soldiered on relentlessly, not wanting to let go?

This tendency to hold on - not give up or let go - is not new to me. I am a chronic serial finisher and cannot give up easily. You may think that this is a good thing, and many times it is.

In 2002, I set my eyes on becoming a marathoner and signed up for the Seattle marathon. I put all my energy into it and trained hard. A month into my training, I developed stress fractures on both my legs and had to stop running. I couldn't get back to running for another two months. But then I did....and trained for the same marathon again, and - alas - got hurt again. I felt angry and dejected. I had failed before I even got to the start line. But giving up on the dream was not an option. I strengthened my resolve as I was nursing my injury.

Finally - after two mistrials - one July day in 2012, I did it. I completed my first marathon and I felt unparalleled joy and pride. I had got to the summit of my own Everest. This is still an accomplishment that I hold dear to my heart.

It was a good thing I didn't give up on my dream of running marathons. However, there are many times this tendency to never, ever give up is not a good thing. For example:

I finish every book I start no matter how miserable I feel reading it. The number of times I plod through books that evoke in me a keen sense of resentment for the author is countless.

I hold on to material things I buy long after they have lost their usefulness or beauty. At some point, they become clutter and yet I cling on to it.

I strive at projects that I do not have passion for anymore.

But why do I do it? There are several explanations in behavioral science. Humans are generally loss-averse: the pain of losing something is twice as acute as the delight in gaining the same thing when you didn't possess it. We worry about a future where we do not have the things we now have. This future is unknown, and humans fear the unknown. Giving up on something you have nourished for a while also evokes the discomfort *of sunk cost fallacy.* Sunk cost fallacy describes the bewildering mindset we adopt when we do not want to let go of something that we have invested in, even if that investment is not paying off anymore. We continue to increase our investment and tie ourselves up in tangles. Abandoning after you have sunk time and effort into something feels wasteful.

What we don't realize, though, is how loss aversion and holding on to something useless are irrational behaviors. They are leftovers from our primal past, when small losses could mean huge catastrophes. It doesn't help us to make important life choices, misinformed by that baggage.

So how do we overcome these irrational behaviors and get ourselves to let go when necessary? Here is what I have tried that can help:

First, evaluate the activity/relationship/thing you are having trouble letting go of. **When you bring it to mind, what do you feel?** If you do not feel joy – and instead you have worry, resentment, boredom, or any negative feeling – then set an intention to let go of it NOW.

Ask the question that my friend asked: **what is the worst that can happen if you let go?** Will it be a catastrophic loss you cannot recover from? More often than not, this is not true, and you realize it as soon as you ask that question of yourself consciously.

Ask yourself: **if you did not have it with you already, will you go and seek it now?** If you will not, why are you keeping it?

As you think about letting it go, **acknowledge any emotions that come up**. Fear of the future, regret about the past, and anxiety, are natural feelings that can arise, and it is ok for you to feel them. These will dissipate as you feel the freedom of letting go.

Finally, just do the deed: let go.

Some things – like stopping to read a book you hate – may require less effort. Some things – like ending a side hustle, divesting from a project, or leaving a toxic team – may take repeated reflection and meditation. It took a few reflection sessions before I could stop working on my project, but I am happy to say that I did.

In the end, I realized as I was talking to my friend that life is not a ledger to be filled with tick marks against goals and activities. No one is evaluating you for finishing everything you start, regardless of how you feel. Life is meant to be lived well, happily and with meaning. If something you're holding on to goes against that rule, it is time to jettison it.

Trust me – when you do, you'll feel free and joyous.

Some parting thoughts

Life is too precious to stay in toxic situations and do things that do not bring you joy, just because you have already invested time in them.

When dealing with projects you are reluctant to give up, check if you are falling prey to sunk cost fallacy.

12

The Moriartys to our Sherlock

How to deal with difficult people

It happened once again. Jim and I had gone back and forth, and back and forth, on some very minor tactical point. The room was full of people from both our teams, and there was a nervous silence all around. In the silence, Jim's and my voices echoed more stridently than either of us intended. The minutes ticked away on the clock, and we had not come to any productive conclusion. I could feel my heart race and a dull pain was developing in my head. It was almost as though I was under attack.

Jim and I had many common goals, but because of our very different approaches, we often sparred. I used to work with Jim more than a decade ago. He sprang to mind when a mentee asked me a question: How have you evolved your approach to handling difficult personas (peers who don't collaborate) over the years?

Back in the day, I used to think of Jim as a peer who was difficult to collaborate with. This is why he came to mind when my mentee asked me that question. But over the years I have realized that I was mistaken. I had jumped to a conclusion about Jim. I had painted him into a corner in my mind as "uncollaborative" when in fact the situation was more complex.

It is possible for us - especially in the heat of the moment - to rush to a conclusion and personalize blame. Psychologists call it the *fundamental attribution error*: the human tendency to ascribe another person's actions to the kind of person we think he/she is while your ascribing own actions to situational factors. If your spouse spills their coffee on the countertop, it is because "she is always careless" while if you do the same, it is because "you are in a rush to drop off the kids". If Jim didn't play nice, it was because "he was uncollaborative". If I didn't play nice, it was because "I wanted to do the right thing for the team".

To be honest, I don't know many details about my mentee's difficult peer. It may very well be that they are hard to work with and need some coaching. But in most tense scenarios involving two or more people, I have come to realize that there are several ways to approach the conversation and debug the situation.

Emotional: How are you feeling in the situation? How is the other person feeling? Are you being threatened in something you hold dear or vice versa? A wonderful tool to diagnose the emotional angle of the puzzle is the SCARF (stands for Status, Certainty, Autonomy, Relatedness, Fairness – supposedly the five drivers of human motivation) model, invented by Dr. David Rock, the CEO of Neuroleadership Institute. I have started using it more and more over the years.

Logical: This is where presenting your facts and hearing the other person's facts come in. Remind each other of your common goal, and why finding a way to collaborate effectively is important. Present your facts and arguments in a way that appeals to the other person (using stories vs. numbers, e.g.).

Situational: It is important to understand what pressures and agendas the other person has on their mind. A little bit of empathy helps here, and so does active listening to his/her words. You get a lot of insights by "getting on the balcony" and by observing for a while.

Cultural: What sort of processes and culture in the team is enabling the situation? What can be done at a macro-level to effect change?

Personal: Here is where the kind of person you are dealing with comes into the picture. Perhaps the person does need some coaching. Perhaps they are missing some key skills or awareness of how they are coming across.

Debugging the personal factors that contribute to the situation - both for yourself and the other person - has a role to play but, in my mind, only as the last step.

When faced with difficult people or situations at work (or life), my advice to my mentee was to pause, breathe, zoom out, and assess all of the above. The logical angle is really the only thing I got right in my own situation with Jim. At that stage in my career, as analytical as I am, I had missed the other aspects altogether. Thanks to the gravity of what we were trying to achieve together, Jim and I did end up working fabulously together. But if I were to encounter that situation again, I would do it more holistically. It would have helped in avoiding many a stressful moment for both of us, and our teams.

Some parting thoughts

Before jumping to conclusions about people, check yourself for fundamental attribution error. Are you ascribing situational factors to personal faults?

When dealing with difficult people, try to approach your situation from multiple angles: emotional, cultural, logical, situational, and finally personal.

13

Getting on the balcony

Why being quiet in meetings can help

"Who can be silent for five minutes?", a friend had thrown this challenge on the table.

A group of us - friends and colleagues - were out on a happy hour when someone mentioned a silent retreat his friend had been on. In this retreat, everyone had to be silent – no communication, online or offline – from dawn to dusk. A tough challenge for our group, given our conversation never ceased. Casual banter, ribbing each other, laughing hysterically at inside jokes were all part of any evening together.

But two of us took up the challenge. A timer was set, and we became quiet. At the end, though, it was not clear what anyone would gain from intentionally remaining silent for any length of time.

This is when I remembered the idea of "getting on the balcony".

I first encountered the concept of "getting off the dance floor, and on the balcony" at a leadership retreat at Microsoft. The instructor had said: To be an effective leader, you should not always be in the fray or on the dance floor. You need to learn how to be quiet in meetings.

Be quiet in meetings? But how would that help? I described to you, a few chapters ago, how you can control your jitters and speak up more in meetings.

I told you how communicating well can be a true differentiator in your career. So why would anyone want to develop the skill of silence in their professional life?

Here are some reasons why:

1) Humans love to feel heard and understood. Research shows that less than half of anything anyone says is properly understood. But more importantly, only 7% of our communication is verbal. Given these stats, and the importance to relationships in day-to-day life, it makes sense to be quiet and try to carefully understand others first.

2) If you constantly keep throwing your two cents in, people's real thoughts and opinions can get masked or biased. Inclusive environments where everyone's true opinions are heard yield better results. This is especially important if you're a senior leader in an organization, and people could feel an unspoken pressure to "fall in line".

3) Most importantly, you need to be centered yourself to act in emotionally intelligent ways. Our biology is wired to constantly scan our environment for threats and rewards. Any signal goes through our primal brain centers first, and if you do not act from a place of calm awareness, you run the risk of making poor decisions triggered by quick emotional reactions.

You cannot stay on the balcony forever, though. Action is important for progress and most tech corporations are biased toward action. But occasionally stepping on the balcony before acting can lead to better decisions and a healthy workplace.

So how exactly do you get on the balcony? Checking in with yourself is a required first step. You need to understand your emotional state, and regulate it, before you can understand the emotional state of others. I find that taking three deep breaths and focusing inward is a good way to settle in.

Then you observe. Pay close attention to everything happening around you, what everyone is saying and more importantly what they are not saying. Watch their body language and gauge the level of comfort they have in a situation. If needed, lean back physically to signal to your brain that you are stepping out of the fray for a bit.

Resisting the urge to say something and always act is a skill that needs to be learned and kept sharp. Practices like meditation and silent retreats can in fact help develop this skill. The more often you take yourself off the fray, the more easily it comes to you in tense situations.

Next time something intense and important is going on in your team (or your life), get on the balcony. You'll be surprised how different and lucid the perspective is from there.

Here are some things to try

Next time you are in a meeting that is important or getting raucous - too many opinions, too many voices speaking at the same time – remind yourself to get on the balcony for ten minutes. Just observe and process what is going on around you. Then act. This can help you understand the dynamics in the room and the people on your team better.

14

In a room where few look like me

How to feel at home when you are different from others

When I was a girl, my cousins and I used to spend summer breaks together in our grandparents' home. We enjoyed listening to stories from our grandmother, lying close to each other, on her moonlit terrace. At dinnertime, grandma would seat us all on the floor and feed us from the same batch of yogurt rice she had whipped up, mixing creamy curds with cold rice. We memorized movie songs and sang them in synchrony. We strung jasmine flowers, and we gossiped.

We particularly loved dressing up in adult clothes: flowing, bright saris wrapped around our unformed waists. We would wear makeup too: a thick coat of white powder to lighten our skin and brighten our faces, dark kajal to line our eyes, and a dab of plum lipstick on our lips. After we got dressed up, we would preen in front of a dull mirror. We would swish our saris around and stand together for our family to look at and say nice things. We all wanted to be called pretty, to be adored.

One warm summer evening, my older cousin dressed up in a bright red sari and my younger cousin in a jade green one. I was in hot pink. We piled into grandma's living room and were ready to show off. My grandma looked at my two cousins first. Oh, how beautiful you look, she said warmly. The bright red and the jade green saris looked startling on their milky skin. My cousins were pleased. There were smiles all around. Then, my grandma looked at me. She paused, as though searching for the right expression. Finally, she pursed her lips and said: "This hot pink looks too gaudy on you. Your skin is too dark for these bright colors."

She paused again and sighed. "Oh well, you are at least tall, and you are smart."

I was confused. So, I was not as beautiful as my cousins? Is that what my grandma meant? Her words haunted me, and I turned them over and over in my head as I tried to sleep. You see, I was a little girl who prized being good-looking above all else, and I had just learned that I was perhaps not a pretty girl. My cousins were fair-skinned, and many in India adored their pale Bollywood actresses and worshipped fair skin. Dark skin, on the other hand, needed to be lightened with bleach or hidden away underneath coats of light powder. I had skin the color of burnt caramel. In my family, I was a misfit among my light-skinned cousins.

Being a misfit has been my perpetual state in my life. I was a misfit in every home I moved to after my mother passed away, an intruder in every family. I have always been a misfit at work. Someone that sticks out, someone who had grown up in a different culture, a woman of color, a minority. Someone with different perspectives. Perhaps it is exactly because of my origins of never fitting in that I am perfectly at ease with being different at work. When I walk into a room full of people that do not look like me, I do not let that stop me from voicing my perspective. I do not let that stop me from asserting my voice or claiming my share of the time.

With few people looking like me, do I ever feel like I do not belong in these corporate meeting rooms or board rooms? Do I ever feel like an impostor?

Undoubtedly, I do. I feel the infamous impostor syndrome a lot, but that's not because I look different from my teammates. I feel like an impostor when I try to do things at work that are slightly beyond my reach, and I must extend myself to get to them. In that sense, feeling like an impostor is a good thing. It means that I am growing, that I am reaching for difficult things.

And it is not just minorities in tech that feel the impostor syndrome, and that's why I don't think that my impostoring is coming from me being different from others in my field. I have heard white men talk about it too. I worked with a Corporate Vice President at Microsoft who once admitted that he felt like an impostor in his job. He was a salesperson who had become a VP, and being among all the engineering types, he felt like a fraud. This man was very successful in the company, a white guy with a brilliant business mind, and a seasoned leader. And yet, he felt like an impostor.

So, if you are feeling like an impostor, know that it's ok. You are likely doing the right thing. You are uncomfortable because you are trying to do hard things. But do not let that feeling stop you from making progress or airing your thoughts. Quiet that negative inner voice that whispers to you that you're not good enough. To do so, try using mantras like below. These are mantras I've created for myself, and I say them to myself, over and over, whenever I feel that cold clasp of the impostor syndrome around my throat.

"I have the right to my voice and my perspectives."

"I belong at this table."

"I am enough."

If one of these works for you, borrow it. If not, create a mantra of your own.

Another way to deal with impostor syndrome is to sign up to do difficult things that are outside your comfort zone often. Doing big, scary things builds up your reservoir of self-confidence. The more of those you do, the more you succeed and the more you fail. Your failures show you that things are seldom catastrophic, that you will survive to see another day, and your successes build up your confidence.

Companies, especially in tech, should do everything in their power to bring more diversity in. We should strive to create a culture where belonging is easier for everyone, and everyone feels welcome. But if you are on a team where you are different, where no one looks like you, do not sweat it. Being different, being a misfit, can indeed be a superpower, a differentiator. It can get you noticed more. It can add to the overall makeup of the team.

Deal with the inner voices that come in the way of your own power. It doesn't matter if you are a robin among ravens; you have a right to your voice, your space, and your perspectives.

Some parting thoughts

Being different from everyone else is ok. It can help you greatly.

Deal with your negative inner voice using your own mantras. My mantras include, "I am enough", "I belong at this table", and "I have a right to my voice and my perspectives". Reflect on what are yours.

Failures are rarely catastrophic. You will live to see another day.

Sign up to do difficult things. These can help build your self-confidence

15

The art of storytelling and executive presence

How to present your ideas effectively

Y ou might think that the field of technology is all about working with computers. All that "people stuff" – that is for the Humanities. But that would be a mistake.

Technology is very much about people. We build products, services, and experiences for people, with people. We need to be able to appeal to humans with our products. We need to convince leaders of the promise of our ideas and designs. We need to capture people's attention with each of the hundreds of emails we send every year. We need to influence our teams to align with our strategies. We need to be able to connect, educate, persuade, convince, and inspire at various times. Whether it is what you're creating with your code, or ideas in your mind that need to be communicated, knowing how people work and what appeals to them is crucial. All of this requires storytelling skills.

Storytelling has become a hot topic in modern times, and that is not without reason. The world is awash with information and people's attention is constantly splintered. There is less time in our lives than ever before. So, it is critical that you hook your audience quickly and convey what you want to convey clearly. Most engineering schools where a lot of us techies get trained do not train us to become good storytellers. Therefore, we end up being dismal at it.

If you have sat through a presentation where an engineer droned on, getting tangled in the shrubs when she should be showing you an aerial view of the forest, you know what I am talking about. We have all listened to people that ramble, their words scattering in the air like pennies hurled on the floor, not telling any cogent story. Perhaps you have stood in front of a group yourself, seeing the glazed eyes and bored expressions of your audience. People whipping out their phones and the influencers in the room tuning you out. How do you avoid being that person that loses or confuses people? How do you effectively articulate your ideas, your tech, your stories?

Like many, I didn't receive training in school for this. I was one of those rambling, mediocre presenters with no clue about storytelling. However, after I started presenting at Microsoft, I received a lot of feedback. Some of this feedback came from my managers and mentors. Some came from professional speaking coaches. I learned some more tips on my own, by watching other spellbinding presenters do their magic. Over time, I got better as a speaker. I am still not an outstanding one, but I can sustain my audience's attention, and I am constantly improving. I know that, If I can become a good presenter, anyone can.

So, how can YOU give a good presentation at work? If you do an online search on "how to do great presentations", you will find a plethora of opinions on it. There are some great books dedicated to the topic, and I have listed them in the Resources chapter of this book. Here are some of my tips, gathered from my experience.

1) First, think about Why you Are Presenting

Author and speaker Simon Sinek titled his bestseller book "Start with Why". I cannot agree more. While Sinek gives this advice to help leaders motivate their teams better, it is great advice for most things we do in life. Meditating on why we are doing it – why am I writing this book, why you are giving that talk, why I am signing up for this class etc. – gives us the kind of clarity that makes every subsequent thing go smoother and be aligned with a true purpose.

There are many reasons people give talks. Some talks persuade people to act. Some inspire, some inform audiences of new developments, and some educate. Think about your presentation and what outcome you want to drive with it.

2) Next, Think about your audience. Who are you Talking to?

When we start building products, as technologists and entrepreneurs, we start with People. Who is the customer for this product? What does she look like? What is the key to her world? What does she care about, day in day out? What are her challenges, her worries, her joys? The more we know about our customer, the better our product will suit her.

Likewise, when you are giving a talk to a group of people, think about the profile of your audience. I routinely ask event organizers about the size of the crowd they are expecting. What is the mix of people like – their experience levels, their expertise, and so on? I think about what will surprise this audience, what will jolt them out of their seats, what will cause them to pay attention to what I am saying. What will cause strong reactions in them, and what questions they could have as I present my material to them. All this reflection about the audience will help you speak in the language that appeals to them.

But what if the audience is diverse? Who do you then tailor your talk to? That depends on why you are giving the talk. If it is to inform the greatest number of people in the crowd, then tailor your talk to appeal to the majority. If you want to get influential stakeholders in the room to consent to something, or be your ally in something, then appeal to the influencers. But, truly, deeply, know your audience.

3) How do you lay out your content?

Once you understand the why and the who, it's time to think about the what. Storytelling has had a long tradition. Since the days of the Paleolithic humans who took it upon themselves to paint cows and horses on cave walls, we have been storytellers. As a result, we know many things about good storytelling.

Well-told stories have an arc. First there is the **windup**, where we describe the current state of the world. We talk about what is the problem with the status quo, what is the hurdle we are trying to jump over. Then we talk about the **opportunity** – what is the benefit to the team, the business, or the company if we try to get over this **hurdle**. Here we may want to discuss how others in the market have addressed this problem – a competitive analysis. Then comes our **vision**, what would the world be like after we have solved this issue. Our vision can be achieved in many ways, of course, so we outline two to three **options**. We talk about the pros and cons of each of these options. We close with the one option we are recommending and discuss the fine print **details** like timelines, resources needed, any early validating signals we have for the idea and so on. Presentations that have concrete asks or **calls for action** to the audience leave them with something to do when they leave the room.

Every story should start with a hook. A hook can be a question that invites your audience to participate, or a request for them to imagine a scenario. It could be a stunning statistic, the dangling of a carrot, so to speak. It could be something that gets them to laugh genuinely or a captivating human story. Think about why your audience will want to pay attention to you for the next few minutes or hours. This can help you craft a good hook.

If you are using slides, do not cram them with words. This is one of the worst ways to present a story. While you are saying something, the audience will be trying hard to read the words on the slides instead. Their attention will now be split across listening to your words and processing those on the screen. Treat your audience kindly and avoid wordy slides. Instead, use pictures where you can. Again, not too many pictures, especially not pictures with quotes and words. Keep the visuals simple and clean.

Being in the field of technology, surrounded by analytical people, we will often need to present numbers to make our case. But make sure you are not throwing data on the screen like you are spreading seeds to the wind. You will just be increasing the cognitive strain for your audience if you do that. They will work their brains hard to make sense of it all, and hence lose you. Try to extract insights from the data and present the insights.

Keep tabs on your use of jargon. Especially if you are talking to a diverse group of people, remember that not everyone knows everything that you know. Above all, keep the human at the center. You are talking to humans about technology that you are building for humans. Every chance you get, bring empathy and the human element into your storytelling.

4) How do you deliver the content?

Now that you have your talk ready, let's focus on the how. How you deliver your talk influences how much of the audience's attention you can retain. What are some tips to deliver your talk well and have a great stage presence?

If you have a stage, use it well. If you are presenting in a conference room, try to stand up while presenting. The center part of the room or the stage is the best spot to command attention but move around if you can. That doesn't mean you pace nervously. That can be distracting. But move intentionally through your speech. If you have three distinct segments to your talk, say, move to a different part of the stage for every segment.

Talk to the humans in the room, instead of an abstract "room". Make eye contact and sustain the eye contact for a few seconds before you move to the next person. Connect and interact with your audience. Typical strategies here include pointing to someone and asking a benign question, polling the audience, and so on. If you have a physical object that can draw their gaze – a mobile phone, a book, a sheet of paper – that you can hold up to make a point, do so. Props help in engaging the audience. Plan and practice your transitions, from one slide to another, or one part of your talk to another. Without proper transitions, you are just presenting disparate parts of your talk without a connecting story arc.

Slow your delivery down and pause generously. Pause more often than you think you should. People that are trying to process what you are saying are working hard mentally, so give them the space to do so without stress. Remember to take one deep breath between every sentence or every other sentence. Get rid of your fillers. The uhs, the ums, the likes. They can be annoying, especially if they are repetitive. Do not dwell on any of your screw-ups. Chances are high that no one noticed them except you. No one knows the perfect statement that you wanted to say in your head.

And finally, remember to smile, loosen up, and have fun.

5) And what about those online presentations?

Work is becoming increasingly remote and geo-distributed. As a result, our presentations are becoming more and more virtual. We really don't have a stage or even a room full of our audience anymore. We are crouching in our seats, alone in our own office, trying to land a talk with an audience spread around the world, miles away from us. How do we do this well?

For online talks, first off, turn your camera on. Make sure you are centered on the screen and looking into the camera. Slow down and pause for questions. Make the talk more informal. You do not have a big room and your image is getting funneled through small rectangles on your audiences' screens. This is not a forum to be grand and dramatic, but you will lose the audience if you are monotonous. So, do leverage and modulate your voice. Ask questions of the audience in the beginning and reengage them often. Become comfortable with awkward pauses, and do not rush to fill in every bit of whitespace in the call.

Other than these, most of the advice for physical, in-person presentations apply to virtual talks as well. Remember that online presentations increase fatigue for your audience. So, go very slow, keep it simple, keep it fun, allow for bio-breaks in long sessions, and end your meeting on time.

Some parting thoughts

Contrary to popular belief, people building technology – engineers, program managers – need storytelling skills.

We use storytelling to persuade people of our ideas, to educate and inform, and to inspire.

Anyone can get better at storytelling. Humans have been storytellers for tens of thousands of years, and we can all learn to master the art.

16

Proposals, memos, and email

How writing can help you in your tech career

I grew up with a father that wrote every day. He would wake up at five every morning, the dark of the night still pressing on us, and frogs in the wasteland next to our flat croaking loudly. He would sit cross-legged like a yogi in our living room, place a 1'x1.5' teak plank across his lap, place his notebook on the plank, uncap his Hero pen, and write. From my room, I would hear the scratch of his fountain pen on paper, my grandma snoring in her bed, and the frogs croaking away. My dad wrote many things: poems, essays, short stories, and op-ed pieces for local newspapers. Most of what he wrote, however, no one read. They would lay without a whisper between the lined pages of his bound notebook. This didn't matter to him. He wrote because he HAD to write. He sent some of his creations to magazines and newspapers. Some he would read to me on warm evenings under moonlight and ask for feedback.

I was no stranger to writing when growing up. From a very young age, I wanted to write. From a very young age, I had a love for words and books.

I read a lot in the years I lived in Canada: everything from Virginia Woolf to Richard Dawkins to Vikram Seth to Natalie Goldberg to Douglas Adams. I started writing frequently for local magazines, just like my father had done back home. Writing, I realized was a pleasant activity, but getting my writing published was HARD WORK! I wrote the first drafts, and then reviewed and revised and reviewed and revised multiple times. I spent hours on a 1000-word essay that a magazine would ultimately pay me $100 for. I was not going to make a living as a writer, I decided. Still, I read a lot of books on writing, wrote every day, and continued to strive to become a good writer. My academic writing got a vigorous shine when I submitted my dissertation to my advisor. Every line in my thesis was analyzed, the veracity and the logic of it questioned. The first draft of my thesis was returned with so many red markings that the pages looked like a murder scene.

WHY I WRITE (AND WHY YOU SHOULD TOO)

Obviously, my early years with a writer father had an influence. But I have come to appreciate writing for its multiple benefits to my work and life:

1- **Writing clearly helps you think clearly**. You refine your logic and your arguments by seeing them spelt out on paper.

2- **Communicating ideas has become as critical to work in the information age as using arrows would have been to our ancestors**. At work, you will write many things. Technical documents, business proposals, emails, product vision, and so on. The practice of writing daily helps you organize your ideas to communicate them better.

3- **Writing helps you sharpen your fo**cus. When you sit down to write, and face the tyranny of the blank page, you have no choice but to focus. With practice, this focus gets stronger and transferable to other areas of your life.

4- **Writing is a channel for the dammed river of creativity inside you**. Humans are driven to create. Whether we create a delicious meal for our family, or the Sistine Chapel, the drive to create and the joy of creating is integral to human experience. Writing is an accessible outlet for that creativity.

5- **Writing helps you conquer your fear of rejection**. Over my years of professional experience, I have learned that many of us battle with a fear of rejection so strong it threatens to eat us alive. Every time you write something to be read by others, you put yourself out there for critique and rejection. But by doing so, you learn to deal with the inner talk that tries to stop you because it doesn't want you to be rejected. You learn to quiet it to a mere hiss you can then ignore in other activities in your life too.

6- **Writing helps you share your experiences and the knowledge gained from them**. Language evolved not just so our ancestors can collaborate and kill a mammoth. Language helped us share our experiences with each other. This sharing helped us learn, entertain, and influence action - all things you can do with writing.

7- **There is a philosophical school of thought that consciousness is really self-consciousness**. I.e., you notice yourself as a being because others notice you as a being. Whether you agree with this philosophy or not, there is almost a primal need we have to be heard, to matter to others, to leave behind something of yourself. Writing helps you do that.

I can shake off everything as I write; my sorrows disappear, my courage is reborn. — Anne Frank

I RECOMMEND THAT YOU Take up A WRITING Practice TOO.

The first step is to develop a practice of writing frequently. Every day if possible. You don't need to get a degree in literature to get started. Writing classes and workshops can help but are not necessary. You don't need to comb through the shelves of a library to research a topic.

What do you write about and where do you write? You can start with yourself and your lived experience. And you can start writing just for yourself in your journal. This, in fact, can be stupendously clarifying, and helpful for your mental peace.

You can write about what you're most familiar with. But as you write more, try to delve deeper into your experience. Try to look at it from different perspectives and get to the nugget of truth that is not obvious. Think: what is it that you want your reader to take away after they give you their precious attention? Are you trying to persuade them to do something? Are you trying to teach? Are you trying to just let them see the world from a different lens? Make your point clearly and as powerfully as you can. This skill, practiced over and over, can come in handy as you write your corporate documents and emails.

But all of this will not happen right away. When you start writing, you may find yourselves well and truly stuck. How do you unstick yourself? Anne Lammott, a writing coach, sets out two important activities for writers in her seminal book "Bird by Bird".

- **Writing "Shitty First Drafts"**. Your first draft should be to just get your thoughts on the page. For your second draft, you can do surgery on your first draft and get the piece to do what you want it to do. Your final draft is about fixing up minor things to make it shipshape.

- **Doing short writing assignments**. I often come to my writing space, power up the computer, open Word, and stare. I don't know to what to write or where to begin. To get out of this, I tell myself that my job is to just write one short paragraph. Just a description of my father as he sat writing in our flat all those years ago. That's it.

These two tools have helped me a great deal. In addition, I use "outlining" to help me plan the structure of my work ahead of time. Of course, after I start writing, I let the flow take me in directions I hadn't planned, but I find it good to have some guardrails and mileposts.

When I sit down to write, I do not say to myself, 'I am going to produce a work of art.' I write because there is some lie that I want to expose, some fact to which I want to draw attention, and my initial concern is to get a hearing.
— George Orwell

Some tips on writing at work

At work, of course we don't write novels and memoirs. Most of the time, we write visions, business proposals, reviews, designs, and emails. In this kind of corporate writing, coherency is crucial. Like your presentations, which we discuss in the chapter about storytelling, your writing should have a narrative arc. You should remember that people have very limited time and even more limited attention span, so you should keep your writing clear and concise. Each statement and each paragraph should follow the previous one logically. You should be intentional about the outcome you are after. Your writing should cater to the needs and the knowledge level of your readers. If you are presenting complex data, you should clarify your insights. If you are pitching an idea, you should follow a narrative arc that is powerful – emotionally and intellectually – to move your audience.

Whether you are writing to tell a story to your team or to influence the leaders in your organization, writing is essential to your work and career progress. The more you write outside of your work, the better your communication at work will become.

It doesn't cost much to write and to practice writing. You need just a few sheets of paper and a pen. So, what is stopping you from learning to become a good writer, and therefore a good communicator?

Some parting thoughts

As a techie, you might not think it, but writing helps your career. You learn to process information better and communicate better.

Communication is essential for climbing the corporate ladder and is even more essential as occupy very senior positions in your organization.

Create a regimen of writing every day.

Whether it is a blog post, or a document, or an email, write your "shitty first draft". This will help you dump your mind on paper. Then you edit, revise, and bring more coherency to your text.

Write short things first. The key is to create something on paper frequently so you can keep your pencils sharp.

17

First impressions on your job

How to make difficult career decisions

I have a job that I like, but I have this other job offer/role that is pretty tempting. Should I accept it and move? And, if I do, how do I start off right on the new team?

Have you ever pondered questions like these? I hear them often in my conversations with friends and colleagues.

Change happens in work life for various reasons. The world is teeming with exciting opportunities, and you might have a new one in front of you. Your current job might be getting old, or burning you out, or at risk of disappearing. Whatever the reason, you will likely face the question of change at some point or the other in your life. I have changed teams or roles many times, even though I have worked in just two companies over the course of my career spanning almost two decades. How do you make good decisions about such changes, and what should you do in your new job to land feet first?

Let's begin with the first question.

SHOULD I ACCEPT A NEW JOB/ROLE AND MOVE AWAY FROM WORK I LIKE?

If you hate your current job, it's a no-brainer. Move if you think that the new job is going to be better. Life is too fleeting for you to stay in unhappy or toxic situations. It can be hard to tell if a new job is going to be better than the current one. There are no guarantees, of course, but you can get a sense by talking to the hiring manager, researching online, interviewing people currently on the team, and so on. In any case, your decision-making is generally easier if your current job is not a great one.

But let us say your current job doesn't suck. Then what do you do? In my day job, most of what I do is make decisions for the company and my team. I am quite familiar with how agonizing such important decisions can be. There are too many thoughts jostling in your head to be heard at once. Different possibilities with different outcomes. It can all be very confusing. So, let us talk a bit about decision-making, in general.

Most decisions we make in our lives do not require a lot of thought

Do I want to eat chocolate ice cream or tiramisu cake for dessert?

Do I wear a bright print dress or denim and t-shirt?

Do I want to read fiction or non-fiction next?

Do I *really* want to floss today?

These are decisions that require very little cognitive skill and cycles. They are simple and generally not costly. We make them mostly by how we feel, and it is best not to waste a lot of energy on these pedestrian decisions. People have suggested creating systems and habits in place to aid in making them quickly (e.g.: always pick the piece of clothing closest to you to wear, alternate fiction and non-fiction, always floss after you brush etc.).

There are other decisions that require deep thinking

There are some decisions we make in life - like the question, "should I accept a new role or stick with the current one", that require thought. We make such decisions many times in our lives, so it is best to understand some tools and tips to make them well.

For such decisions, we use two different ways of discernment. The first and the most obvious one, the one that comes naturally to those of us trained in critical thinking, is **deliberation**. i.e., we think. We analyze. We list pros and cons. We use decision-making frameworks. For example, when I deliberate on this topic myself, I consider the following questions.

1. What draws you to the new job? What is the pull? Is it money, is it an opportunity to learn something new, to make something wonderful?

2. Have I done all I can in my current role? There are a few reasons why I think about this question. Firstly, in general, I should not leave my current team in a lurch. This can lead to bridges getting burned to embers – a bad idea for my career. By being thoughtful about quitting, I maintain hard-earned and highly valuable relationships. Secondly, when we face challenges, a part of us eggs us on to quit. It might be the path that requires the least effort. An alternative is to face those challenges and learn from them. Asking myself this question – have I done all I can – helps me get to the bottom of it.

3. How would I rate this job on the things I care about in Work in general? For me, it is important to work with great people, in a culture that aligns with my values, to make a difference to others with my work, to have influence to make changes, and to learn new things constantly. How does this offer stack against those considerations?

4. What does success mean to me at this place? Another way to ask the same question: Is there an exit strategy? What are the boxes that need to be checked by this job, and if not checked, I should look for something else?

5. Can I see any obvious issue with the role? What are the disadvantages I can list?

6. What is my plan if I spectacularly fail in the job? And what does failure mean? It is good to spend a few minutes thinking about this question and the previous one. The goal is not to get discouraged from making the change because there are some disadvantages and possibilities of failure. It might still make all the sense in the world to go for it. But I can use these insights to negotiate my offer better and/or to shape my plan for my first days in the new role.

The second and the more ignored way to answer the question of "should I move to a new job?" is to use the emotional fabric in your mind and your **intuition**. Asking yourself how you feel about it.

Malcolm Gladwell opens his famous book *Blink: The power of thinking without thinking* with the story that underlines the importance of intuition in decisions. He talks about *kouros*, an ancient Greek statue that the Getty Museum was evaluating for a purchase. The asking price for the statue was $10 million. Every scientific analysis on the statue checked out. The art was pronounced authentic and sold for an exorbitant price. However, an art historian who later viewed the statue was struck instantly by the feeling that something was wrong. He felt that it was a fake. A few more art experts that viewed it felt the same too. After more investigations, it was concluded that the kouros was in fact not genuine. The moral of the story is that what weeks of initial investigations could not find was ferreted out intuitively by experts. This is because the experts were able to instantly access a lot of subconscious information in their heads collected over years of learning. It is advisable to not ignore what that trove of information points to.

When making your own personal decisions, therefore, do not ignore that quiet whisper of intuition. It might be telling you something vital. Intuition is a set of mnemonics your brain has stored away from years of learning. A lot of this learning is subconscious, and you are unable to access it consciously and deliberately. But it is important to not undervalue that learning. That said, while intuition is fast, it can be flawed too (as behavioral scientist Daniel Kahneman expounds in his wonderful book *Thinking Fast and Slow*), so sift through what it points to for inherent biases.

As you evaluate your new role, use both these pathways - rational and intuitive - to make your decision.

No matter what conclusion you come to, know that most decisions are reversible.

Most decisions we make in life do not indenture us to them. We can go back and make a different choice, the only loss in most cases being time/money. When you weigh the loss of time/money against the opportunity in front of you, it is likely you come out ahead by deciding sooner than later. Most of the time, which way you go is less important than what you do down the line.

So, simplify consciously. Pick a path, decide on the checkpoints where you want to evaluate how you're doing, have a strategy to roll back or course correct if things are not going as well as you expected. Then make the decision and go on your merry way.

Kahneman says it is best to judge the quality of your decisions not based on how they turned out. If you do that, you fall victim to what is called the *outcome bias.* The world is complex and so many factors are at play that are not probabilistic and not in your control. Judge the quality of your decisions on the process you used to make them. If you used a sound process, you made a sound decision, regardless of the outcome.

Now let's look at the next question.

HOW CAN YOU DO WELL IN THE FIRST DAYS AT THE JOB?

As you start your new job, think about what your strengths are and how you can lean on them to bring value to your team. Reflect on why you were hired. Was it your tech skills, your ability to grow ideas, your professional network, or something else? Make sure you have a plan to leverage them in your job.

Make a list of things you want to accomplish in your first hundred days. Why hundred days? World leaders frequently get reviewed on their first hundred days in office, and this is a great timeframe for your work as well. Three months plus a few days give you enough time to expand your knowledge, learn about the culture, increase your network, get some early wins, and craft long-term goals. As you prepare for your first hundred days, plan your learning. Think about where you can bring quick wins to establish your credibility. Make it a priority to talk to people on the team. Be curious about the business and the technology. Be curious about the humans around you and their stories. Try to connect with them and understand what they do, what they enjoy, and what their challenges are. Doing this will help you learn more, but also build a web of positive relationships around you.

Someone recently asked me if I thought first impressions at a new job were important. Indeed, people make instant judgments based on first impressions. Whether you are making a business deal or interviewing for a role or are in a new job, you will want to think about what story you're telling about yourself when people meet you. People will update their mental models as they get to know you and (hopefully) not rely solely on first impressions, but you want to start off on the right foot. The best way to do that is to be genuine, curious, and empathetic to the people around you.

Changes - in life and at work - are equal parts exciting and challenging. Having a plan to navigate through them, while understanding that no plan will be perfect - and that's ok, you'll adapt - is vital. If you are contemplating a change at work, approach it deliberately. Make a plan and follow through.

Good luck.

Some parting thoughts

When you face an important career question, use a systematic decision-making approach to see what you want to do.

Use both emotional and rational parts of your brain for decision-making.

Most decisions in life are reversible, so do not agonize and overthink them.

As you take on a new role, have a plan for the first hundred days. Plan to get some quick wins and establish long-term goals. Expand your network and immerse yourself in learning.

18

The Secret of Success

What you need to focus on for career success

People love to ask: what is the recipe for career success? What does it take to be spectacularly, thrillingly successful? How can I get recognized at my job? Are there any shortcuts?

I get asked this question many times in my speaking engagements and my mentoring conversations. How did I do it in my own career?

Firstly, I have found no shortcuts to success. Sorry to break your bubble there, but it is true. I have also found that a lot of advice that gets passed around for career success, especially for women and other minorities in tech, is atrocious. Often, women are told they should find female mentors to guide them. They are told to network more and speak more in meetings. Assert themselves for promotions.

Mentorship, networking, being vocal, and advocating for oneself all have their place. I am not against them. In fact, for many of us quiet people, this advice and these reminders are essential. But I also feel sad that most women's conferences and other events focused on underrepresented populations in technology focus solely on this advice. In contrast, here is what I have found in my career.

Career success encompasses four ingredients.

Passion

You need to be passionate about what you are doing at work. I am not saying that you should be chirpy all the time you are in the office, but you should be enthusiastic about your job. Without passion, curiosity, or interest, you will not bring your best game to work. You will not look around for opportunities that can benefit your team or your customers. You will not be driven to learn new things and look for new ways to solve problems. You will simply not be engaged.

Lack of engagement at work is a death knell for your career. So, if you ever find yourself in work that is not evoking any passion in you, think about changing your job. You can either change your job by moving to a new team or a new company, or redesign your work to include things that can help you bring out that passion. Do you like working with people but your job is mostly coding? Can you ask to be on customer visits to bring more of the customer angle to your coding work while also getting to interact with people? Do you like to help others and you can't see a direct link for helping others in your job? How about signing up to mentor the newcomers on your team? Sparking energy and enthusiasm within you for your job is an important part of success.

Excellence

There is no substitute for excellence at your job. You must keep looking for opportunities to become better at what you do. Continue to hone your craft. Pay attention to the details. Learn every day: learn from books, from your job, from people around you, from online courses, from your own successes and failures. Know that mastery will take time and you must stick with it. Every butterfly looks like a caterpillar before it grows into its astonishing beauty. You will likely look bad before you can become brilliant. But your job, indeed, is to continue to work toward becoming brilliant.

Value

Do you know how your work is adding value to your team, to your company, to your customers? If you don't, finding that out should be item number one on your to do list. Talk to your manager and other stakeholders about it. It is critical that you understand why you are doing your tactical tasks, and how they accrue to the company's bottom line and customer value. Occasionally, you will find yourself working on a "grunt project" – some initiative whose outcomes no one really values. You do that either because you are passionate about something that is not core to your organization's strategy or because your manager has thoughtlessly lined you up with something that is not impactful. I do think it is okay for you to be on projects that are not impactful now and then. But most of your energies should be spent on work that is core to your company/team's business.

Exposure

If you were a moviemaker, you would never do this: create a movie and tell no one about it. That might be a way for you to channel your creative energies, but it is not a path to your success as a moviemaker. To have success in your career, you should become comfortable with shining light on your own work. I know many people that are simply not okay tooting their own horn. For many of us, especially the quieter and underrepresented folks in our workplace, promoting their own work doesn't come naturally. We shy away from it.

Here is a formula that sums this up.

Success = (passion plus excellence plus value) times exposure.

If you're bringing zero exposure to your work, the entire equation adds up to zero. So, find a way to advocate for your work. You can talk about the customers that the work benefits, for example. You can talk about the team that you did the project with. You can find a colleague that talks about your work for you, and you can talk about his work in return. These are all ways in which you can avoid talking about yourself. But rest assured, people – especially key influencers in your org – should be exposed to your work for you to see career success.

So, there you go. Those, in my mind, are the ingredients of success.

I know that success means different things to different people, and different things at different points in a person's life. In the beginning of my career, all I was after was financial independence. Now I look more to the value part of that equation. To make a difference in the world. But regardless of what I am after, passion, excellence, value, and exposure are always aspects to which I pay attention. Pay attention to these, and you will find career success.

Here are some things to try

Think of your own work at this moment.

Are you passionate about what you're doing?

Is it bringing value to your company and your customers?

Are you building skills and expertise in your role?

Are you bringing exposure to your work?

If you cannot answer yes to all of the above, you have work to do.

What are three things you can do in the next couple of weeks to fill the gaps you find through your reflection?

Some parting thoughts

Success can mean different things to different people, and different things to you at different points in your life.

Success includes four components: passion, impact, skills, and exposure.

19

The power and joy of attention

Why attention to detail is important

When I was a graduate student in Canada, I got very curious about the religions of the world. I explored the philosophies of many including Hinduism - the religion I was raised in - Christianity, Islam, and Buddhism. I picked up their ideas, held them up to light, and put aside the ones that did not make much sense to me. The concepts and practices of Buddhism in particular enthralled me. Meditation was an important practice in Buddhism, and I wanted to understand it better. One day I decided to join a local community of Buddhist meditators.

I began to drive daily to a dingy second floor apartment in East Vancouver, where about eight of us gathered to spend a few minutes in complete silence. We would kneel on soft off-white cushions placed against the wall. The paint on the wall was a dull white too and had been chipped in many places. We would flutter our eyes half-shut at the clang of a dull gong and stay in stillness for 20 minutes. Then the gong would go off again, and we would get up and gather in the center of the room.

The leader of the group would bring in a pot of hot jasmine tea along with eight little ceramic cups. In the silence of the room, the clatter that the cups and the pot made against the hardwood floor would echo. Then, the leader would take up the pot from the floor and pour out tea into the cup of her neighbor to the left. The neighbor would accept the cup with a bow, place it down, take the pot herself, and fill tea for her neighbor to the left. And on and on we went around the circle, filling tea for our neighbors and accepting our own cups with gratitude. When everyone's cup was filled, we would silently lift our cups to our lips and breathe in the delicate scent of jasmine. We would feel the heat seep from the liquid to the ceramic to our palms, listen to the drone of the heater in the apartment, and notice the steam curl up in front of our faces. We would take tiny sips, all the while paying attention to nothing but the tea and how it warmed our bodies on those cold and clammy winter evenings in Vancouver. Someone would then read Buddhist scriptures, and the evening would end in a series of prostrations, bowing, and circling of a statue of the Buddha, in synchrony.

I was part of this meditation group for a single winter. There came a time when the ritualist aspects of the group started to rankle me, and I stopped going. Two aspects of that experience, however, stayed with me:

I found the practice of meditation to be highly therapeutic and spiritual. I continued meditating at home – sans the circumnavigations of the statue – and still do so almost every day.

Those tea sessions stayed with me. I was impressed by how much the practice stressed paying attention to the tiniest of details.

The tea ceremony came back to my mind when I recently decided to go for a long walk on my neighborhood trail. I have run miles and miles on that trail for years now, and I had hardly registered the details on it. As I slowed down to a walk last weekend and forced myself to pay attention, my environment started to come alive. I saw the first cherry blossoms of the season, blooming in a riotous explosion of pink and white. I noticed the lime green weeds, grass, and moss growing with abandon on all surfaces including the muddy canal by the side of the trail. I heard the incessant warbling of songbirds and the tap-tap-tap of a lone woodpecker. The touch of cold breeze on my cheeks was refreshing.

These details had, however, become a blurry backdrop to my daily runs. **It is so with many other things in life too.**

We often move too fast through our activities - our dinners, our commutes, our work, our conversations with our loved ones – for us notice much of what's going on. We move from pillar to post, scarcely paying attention.

But paying attention is important. Details are important.

Details add color and wonder to our lives. After a long day of humdrum, have you ever looked up at the sky at dusk and been overwhelmed by the flamboyant reds of the sunset? Have you looked at a newborn child's tiny toes curl in on themselves and marveled at how this new life is here now when it was nothingness before? Noticing these tiny details about life and nature gives us a sense of wonder. It makes us realize what a fabulous thing life is. Without these astonishing details, our days can run on, one into another. Our lives can become monotonous.

Details make us better at work and life. If you are a programmer, you should care about your craft deeply. Paying attention to every single line of code and how well they come together can help you write better code. If you want to be a good leader for your team, you should pay attention to every single person on the team – to what excites them, what brings them down, and how they are feeling. If you want to be a good partner or a good parent, you should listen to your loved ones keenly and care about the smallest details of their lives. Details can make an explosive difference to the quality of your work and life. Steve Jobs is reputed to have obsessed over the tiniest details of the products Apple shipped. He cared about even the parts that a customer could not see. He agonized over the exact shade of yellow on the Google logo as seen on an iPhone. There are music composers, painters, sculptors, chefs, and fashion designers that are legendary for their attention to detail.

Details make us happy. Caught up in ourselves and our anxieties, we can often become pre-occupied and unhappy. We brood about the past or worry about the future. We become self-absorbed. But if we stopped and paid attention to the present moment – to how the winter air feels sharp on our skin or how the cool of the water is refreshing on a hot summer day – we can get out of our own heads. Getting out of our heads is a good first step to happiness.

Attention is the rarest and purest form of generosity.

— Simone Weil

It is a myth that greatness is in the big things – monumental discoveries, audacious projects, thrilling adventures, and stupendous triumphs. In our raucous modern world, the quiet whisper of minutiae feels unglamourous and uncool. But it is in these details that success and happiness lie. So next time you have dinner, instead of wolfing it down in front of the TV in ten minutes, try to slow down and pay attention to the flavors. If you are out on a walk at twilight, gaze at the sky. When you are writing a document, pause for a few minutes – perhaps even move to a different task altogether before you come back – and then reread what you have written. Carefully look over the details and make sure the text will make sense to the intended audience. I bet that your happiness, the quality of your work, and the joy in your life will multiply. It is in details that we find the stuff of life and beauty.

20

Work lessons from a superhero

What Wonder Woman can teach us about work

I get it, the expectations were sky-high. The year 2020 was horrendous. A pandemic raged throughout the world. Millions of people died. There was unrest in Hong Kong, in the United States, in Nigeria. When 2020 was not horrendous, it was as exciting as a beige wall. We were closeted in our homes, not being able to travel. Simple pleasures like eating popcorn drenched in butter, in a theater, were denied to us. We deserved some riveting entertainment for our Christmas break. Many of us expected the movie Wonder Woman 1984 that was released that Christmas to be that kind of entertainment. Something that transported us away from our ennui and agonies.

For some of us, the movie delivered.

I found myself spellbound by it. Right from the opening scene when an astonishingly self-confident young Diana Prince, a little girl with plump cheeks, sprints across the green mountains of her homeland, past susurrant waterfalls, to compete with women twice her age, I was all in. Hans Zimmer's music got my heart to soar. I felt pure joy whenever Diana transformed into Wonder Woman and twirled her golden lasso.

I found a few lessons, too, in the movie. Lessons that are valuable for us to remember for work and life. What are those lessons? Here they are.

1. KNOW WHAT YOU LONG FOR, AND WHAT YOU'RE GIVING UP IN RETURN. We have heard the classic tales of greed gone awry. Faustian bargains where what is given up is more valuable than what is acquired. Midas' wish to turn everything he touches to gold nearly starves him to death. Dorian Gray's longing for eternal youth leads him to lies and murder.

Unquenchable and destructive greed is the central moral of WW84, and one that cannot be more relevant to us in our corporate world. As professionals, we can become inveterate box-checkers. Buy a home. Check. Get promoted at work. Check. Get another home. Check. Get promoted again. Check. Get your first million. Check. Get another million. Check.

Though some of this ambition is healthy, it never stops. The hunger for more intensifies and can lead us down some unhappy paths. All the while, we unthinkingly sacrifice our health, the time we can spend with our loved ones, our personal passions, maybe even our legacy. We need to pause and think about what we long for and what we're giving up in return in this bargain.

2. EVERYONE HAS A BACKSTORY. BE CURIOUS AND EMPATHETIC.

Most superhero movies I watch are thoughtless shows of power. Gunshots and explosions almost tear the screen apart. In most of them, heroes embody pure good and villains embody pure evil. There are few nuances and few attempts made to humanize these black and white caricatures.

In WW84, we learn a lot about the backstory of Diana Prince. She becomes a superhero by learning in tough Amazonian wargames and training grounds. We see her disappointments and failures strengthen her. But we also see the villain Max Lord abused by his father and endlessly feeling unworthy of being loved. We see the villain Cheetah simper nervously as an insecure nerd, craving being "more than nothing". The lived experiences of our villains, just like those of our hero, make them who they are. We judge our villains less viciously once we learn what their beginnings were like.

In our work and life, we often come across people that strike us as difficult. But we rarely think about their backstories. I love that WW84 shows us that we should be empathetic to not just the people we like but ones that frustrate us as well.

3. DO NOT BE IN A RUSH TO "BECOME GREAT".

All too often, in our rushed world, we can't wait to be great. Not just be great, but also be recognized as great. But as Antiope warns Diana in the opening scene, this haste doesn't result in excellence. You need to pace yourself, set expectations in your head right, listen, learn, be patient, and progress. Becoming outstanding at anything – whether it is stopping tanks with your bare feet or becoming an admired developer in a software company – is a process and takes time. Bide your time, and do not be in a rush.

4. SHOW RESOLVE TO MAKE HARD CHOICES IN LIFE.

Doing the right thing, sometimes, can be like running up a steep mountain in biting wintry air in the indigo dark of dawn. Uncomfortable, and you really do not want to do it. You would rather stay warm in your bed, tucking your blanket around your toes. And yet, you may need to steel your heart and go on.

In life, such resolve is what will make you great at what you do. When Diana makes her tough choices in the movie, we feel her heart collapse in her chest. But she walks away resolved to move on and face her next steps. That resolve, my friends, is a superpower.

5. BE TRUE TO YOURSELF.

It is better to live in a disappointing truth than a pleasing lie. In the movie Matrix, Neo is offered a choice between a Red Pill and a Blue Pill. The Red Pill will cause him to face a reality that is unpleasant, and the Blue Pill will let him live swimmingly in a blissful make-believe world. Neo chooses the Red Pill. The Truth. Likewise, the Wonder Woman in WW84 urges us to choose Truth. The mirages of wealth, power, fame, and so on can be irresistible, but Truth is what will save your humanity, the movie argues.

What is your truth? What would your life be like if no one was watching (because no one truly is)? Who are you, genuinely? Who do you want to be? Not who you are for the sake of all the mirages in your life, but who do you really want to be? These are all wonderful questions for us to answer as professionals.

I loved WW84 for all these lessons. Unlike other superhero movies, it made me reflect on work and life. Unlike in other superhero movies, too, the hero doesn't just beat people up because she can. She carefully picks apart the innocent people from the guilty ones and avoids punishing the innocent. Such thoughtfulness in the middle of crises is something every leader needs to show.

Unfortunately, the reviews for the movie were largely atrocious. Many people found it to be a disappointment. The pacing felt jittery. There was too much stuff happening and yet not enough. The story was needlessly soapy. Major plot points were inexplicable. I get their disappointment. But personally, the movie was a highlight of my Christmas day. A superhero movie with a female hero that teaches us many lessons for our work and life. What is there not to like?

21

The mirages in your mind

How to avoid the nine thinking traps

I t was the summer of 2018. I had been asked to present some demos at a keynote at Microsoft Inspire. Microsoft Inspire is a massive conference that welcomes over 10,000 attendees every year, most of them IT Professionals, Software Vendors, and System Integrators for big enterprises.

Over 10,000 at the T-Mobile Arena in Las Vegas and close to a million viewers online. I had never spoken in front of such an enormous audience before. So far, my presentations had been in small rooms of a dozen people or in medium-sized All-Hands of around 100 of my own team. I had no clue how to scale up to this size of an audience.

Thankfully, Microsoft came to my rescue. Once I said yes (with trepidation dancing in the back of my head), the team responsible for the keynote put me through some rigorous training. I got a ton of feedback and made several changes to my script. Finally, the big day arrived.

My demo was supposed to last 30 minutes, cycling through many of the offerings in the Microsoft 365 portfolio. I got on stage, energy in my stomach jumping around like overactive molecules in boiling water. The greenroom felt cold. The stage, colder. The blue light shining down on me felt blinding. I couldn't see the audience, not even my friends who were eagerly applauding from the front row. I began my demo.

As I was in the middle of it, walking through a script that I had rehearsed many times before, I knew something was off. The buttons I was expecting on the screen were not there! I had no clue where these buttons had gone off to, and I needed to click on them to flow through my demo. (I learned later that the team had deployed a new version of the code to production.) I stumbled over my words and started to sweat. I could sense over 20,000 eyeballs on me. I felt I was hurtling toward disaster. This was not the smooth landing I had hoped for. I handwaved through the next steps and ended my demo.

I got off the stage and walked to the backroom. As I was walking, a series of thoughts circled through my head: everyone in my leadership likely saw what a bad job I did and was thinking poorly of me; why did I even sign up to this, I was never going to be a great presenter; my entire demo was such a fiasco. And on and on.

When I saw my demo team in the backstage, my shoulders drooped. I told them I was sorry for failing them. What I was met with in return were stares of puzzlement. Turned out, no one had really realized that anything was off, except me. They had all felt that the demo had gone great. When I opened up Outlook on my phone, I saw many notes of congratulations from my colleagues who all said they had loved seeing me on stage and the storytelling. So, why was I so off in my perception of the presentation compared to almost everyone else?

That's because I had just fallen prey to what psychologists call "Thinking Traps". As part of a recent stress management program I undertook through Microsoft benefits, I learned about nine of them.

1. **Fortune telling**: This is when you predict the future, with a strong negative bias. E.g.: "I'll never be a good presenter".

2. **Black and white thinking**: This is also called "all or nothing thinking" - something is either all good or all bad. E.g.: "I made two mistakes in that presentation. It was a disaster".

3. **Mind reading**: Humans - like few other organisms - can try and guess the contents of minds that are not their own. But often we guess wrong. E.g.: "They think I am not a good presenter".

102

4. **Over-generalization**: We tend to take one incident and make something about that all-pervasive or permanent about our lives. E.g.: "I always screw up in presentations"

5. **Labeling**: This is the tendency to attribute overarching character traits based on specific incidents or behaviors. E.g.: "I made two mistakes in one presentation. I am such a bad presenter".

6. **Overestimating danger**: When we take a molehill, build it up into a mountain, and worry about our security, we are falling into this trap. E.g.: "I did a poor job in my talk. I am going to lose my reputation and get fired".

7. **Negative filtering**: Many of us have a predilection for the negative. We zone in on critical feedback and obsess over it 10 times more than praise. We disregard the positives about a situation and fret about the negatives. E.g.: "Everyone was bored. I saw three people in the audience looking at their phones".

8. **Catastrophizing**: Sometimes, when we make small errors, our minds can mislead us to imagine the worst case. E.g.: "Now I went and did it. One day I am going to be an utter failure living under a bridge".

9. **Should and Must statements**: Our lives overflow with "shoulds" and "musts". We rarely question these and try to satisfy them, almost on autopilot. E.g.: "I should always be on and always do a perfect job"

On that sweltering summer day in Las Vegas, I was guilty of at least #2, #3, #4, #6, #7, and #9 on that list.

Knowing about these traps helps us reason over our own automatic thinking patterns. This means that we can now stop ourselves when we get sucked into behaviors that are no good for our mental wellbeing. Stopping and wondering if we are falling into any of these traps short-circuits the default-mode network that drags us into behaviors that we are hardly conscious of. When Descartes said in the 16th century "I think, therefore I am", he didn't have the background that neuroscientists and psychologists have today. We now know from science our brains construct our reality for us. It is therefore super useful to be aware of traps in our thinking so there is a chance of perceiving the world closer to reality.

22

The serendipity of preparation

How fortune favors the prepared

I love low-light photography. The quality of natural light at the right time of day, when the sun is at a low enough angle to light my subjects softly, is just magical. The pictures in this chapter were taken one weekend in Cannon Beach, Oregon, when we got possibly the most spectacular sunset I had ever seen. The sky dazzled with blues and pinks and oranges. I ended up that night with some of the best pictures I have taken ever since I took up photography as a hobby.

But there is more to these pictures than what you see. Here are a few things you DO NOT see:

I had previously read books, followed other photographers, and watched videos to learn the camera work needed for low-light photography and good composition.

I had researched the previous day online for the best spots for sunsets on the OR coast. I had picked the Haystack Rock as where I'd be that evening.

We had driven to the beach earlier in the day to scope out the area for different photography angles.

I had come back to the rock an hour before sunset, dressed in multiple layers and a beanie and gloves, so that I could assess the type of light and the position of tides.

I had foregone the other delightful options that evening to just sit on a blanket and read a book or take in the sunset in the arms of my partner.

I had walked around in cold January seaside weather, lugging my camera and my tripod for an hour and a half, shooting several pictures. Another photographer I met had come even more prepared: he was wearing wellies.

Dozens of these pictures ended up being dull. Only a couple did the grand show of light the justice it deserved.

Sometimes you get good things in life because you are in the right place at the right time. Most times, though, you work to steer yourself into that place at that exact time. In the case of these pictures, serendipity did play a role. The sunset that day was just astonishing, and I couldn't have planned for it. But preparation, vision, passion, determination, an ability to put up with discomfort, prioritization, and a stomach for failure were all part of it too...just like they are part of many opportunities and successes we have in our lives. Often, we see just the things that are visible to us and get misled by how easy someone's success might look. It is important to peel back the layers to understand everything that truly went into it.

23

A bucket of opportunities

How to spot opportunities on the horizon

My very first manager at Microsoft, Colin, gave me some advice that I'll never forget.

It was my day two at the company. I walked into Colin's office for a one-on-one meeting. Among my first questions to him - how can I be successful in this company?

He looked at me, took a breath, and then said these life-changing words.

"Raji," he said, "whenever you walk into my office and ask me for an opportunity, I can give you one from this bucket I have." He mimed holding an invisible bucket in his right hand. "You see, this bucket has a few opportunities I have for all my team. If you deliver on one with quality and on time, you'll do well.

"But...what will really make you excel here is if you brought in an opportunity yourself AND delivered on it. Does that make sense?"

I didn't fully get it then, but I did with time. He wanted me to create new opportunities for myself and for the team. He wanted me to be inventive, creative. To give more than to take. He wanted me to help shape the future for us by actively scanning the horizon. That, in his view and now in mine, is required for doing outstanding work.

I recently shared this advice with someone. She told me it was great advice but asked where she could find these new opportunities. Are there some things she can do to be able to spot them in her horizon?

Here are a few tips that I have compiled for her, and for you.

1. READ WIDELY

If there is a single habit that has helped me leaps and bounds, it is my habit of reading. I read because I enjoy reading. Reading happens to be one of my *hygge* things to do. But reading has also enhanced my career in many ways. I routinely find new ideas in the books I read, whether it is around technology or software engineering or leadership or business. My first suggestion to you is to pick up books on a wide range of subjects. Follow recommendations from folks you admire and leaders in your field. Reflect on your areas of strength and weakness and target your reading toward both. Spend rainy afternoons in bookstores, libraries, or on online catalogs of books. Browse websites and publications like HBR, WSJ, Hacker News, Joel on Software, High Scalability, and Tech Crunch. You might be surprised by where you find that little diamond of information that is very relevant to your work.

2. LISTEN ACTIVELY

It is important to be aware of what is going on in your organization, broadly if not deeply. Try to discern where the "puck is going to be" - the possible landscape of the future. Pay attention - REAL attention - to what people say in meetings, in conversations, and in emails. Be present and keen to learn. Be aware of your own reflexes - the reflex to think of your response before you fully grok what someone is saying, the reflex to quickly dispute a different perspective, the reflex to make assumptions - and challenge them. Focusing your mind becomes easier if you have a daily contemplative practice.

Being plugged in in your organization can give you tremendous advantages.

3. CUT THROUGH THE NOISE

We create 2.5 quintillion bytes of data in a single day. That is an overwhelming amount of information and much of it is not going to help you with your next opportunity. How can you be effective in paying attention to the right things?

Nancy Pearl, a Seattle-based librarian and bestselling author, has proposed

"The Rule of 50" for dropping bad books, books that are not serving your time well. The idea is to give every book a small chance - no more than 50 pages - to interest you. In software engineering terms, "fail fast" on the books you read. It takes roughly an hour to read fifty pages, and for most information that comes our way online - blog posts, Reddit/Twitter threads, emails, and articles - an hour is a lot to give. I'd fail fast within two minutes for such things.

This will help you save your most important resource - your attention - on things that matter the most.

4. MAKE CONNECTIONS

It is not enough to listen mindfully, absorb information from a variety of sources, and have an excellent ability to retain it all. You need to be able to make connections between what you learn and how it is applicable to your work. Making parallels between varied domains is a good path to innovation. You see/hear, understand, and reimagine ideas. This is called *analogical thinking* and it is crucial for finding new opportunities.

"Modern life requires range, making connections across far-flung domains and ideas...Analogical thinking takes the new and makes it familiar, or takes the familiar and puts it in a new light, and allows humans to reason through problems they have never seen in unfamiliar contexts." - David Epstein, author of Range

Many innovators and scientists have been known to do exactly that. In his book Range, Epstein argues that having multiple careers and interests can give professionals more scope for such analogical thinking, resulting in better innovations. One great way to innovate is to bring your previous background and experiences - from another field, another industry - to do something better at your current job.

When you learn something new in a book or an article or a conversation with a colleague, think of the connections you can make to your own work. How can you apply it to something that can help your team or your customers?

5. BUILD RELATIONSHIPS

I am a rank-and-file introvert. Given a choice, I'd rather stay in my large-sized recliner, a thick fleece blanket around my ankles, and my nose in my kindle, than meet new people. But I have come to realize that meeting new people can be both enjoyable and useful in my life and work. You can learn new things from people, learn more about how your work can help them or vice versa. You can build relationships that enrich your life. What's more, studies have shown that social connections can make you happier - even if you are an introvert.

So, these days, I have learned to allow new situations and new people to surprise me. I have put myself forward and done a little bit more of that dreaded "networking" than I'd do naturally.

6. RAISE YOUR HAND

Of course, my manager Colin didn't advise me to just come up with new opportunities for the team. He wanted me to execute on some of them as well.

When there is a new, exciting thing that comes your way, sign up for it. Raise your hand, even if you do not feel like you have everything figured out just yet. Trust that you will figure it out, with patience, time, help, and effort.

Not all opportunities you think of will be celebrated by everyone around you. Some of them will turn out to be gold, and some will be just dust. That's ok. The key is to keep hunting for new ways to shape the future.

24

Driven as a salmon and calm as a heron

How ambitious you should be

I relish my philosophical conversations with my father. They give me a kind of perspective that I often need. My dad quotes to me wisdom from the Bhagavad Gita, Shakespeare, Dale Carnegie, Mahatma Gandhi, and many others. In return, I tell him about the new things I learn from the books I read, and my experiences at work: topics ranging from neuroscience to leadership to human behavior to meaning in life.

In the summer of 2020, my father and I had a conversation about the perpetual dissatisfaction I feel with myself and my life. I told him how, no matter what goals I set for myself and how much success I have in achieving them, my heart is always tinged with dissatisfaction. Here I am, sitting in a spacious home with a partner that loves me, with no worry about where the next meal is coming from, working for a company that I truly believe in...and yet I don't feel satisfied with my life. "Why is that? And what should I do?" I asked.

I am grateful that my dad didn't just dismiss my questions and statements as whining. "You and your problems of privilege," he could have said. Or "Stop overthinking and appreciate your blessings". But he didn't. He listened to me patiently. Then he said that I feel dissatisfied because that is how humans are supposed to feel. Just because we had a wonderful breakfast in the morning doesn't mean we would stop eating at lunch or dinner. We would feel hungry at night, and hungry again the next day. The constant craving and reaching for things will always be there.

"If you stop reaching for things," my father said, "if you stop dreaming about your next goal, your next challenge, that is when you stop living."

That is a spectacular statement to make. But it is one that I find myself naturally drawn to. Despite the numerous reminders from society that ambition is not womanly - a woman needs to put family first, be a mother, be a caring wife/daughter etc. - I nurture within me a strong desire to make a difference in the world beyond myself and my family. It's also no surprise that my dad has that view. Let me tell you a bit about his life.

My father was a little boy in the '50s. When he was growing up, in the traditional Indian style, he lived with his extended family in his uncle's home. His uncle was the patriarch, and my father craved his attention and love. Like many Indian kids, he loved playing cricket with his friends. He loved his mother and his siblings. He loved the English language. From his mentors, he borrowed copies of Shakespeare, Wordsworth, and Thomas Hardy - not to read and enjoy the stories, but to learn new words. In general, he loved standing out and being excellent. He entered every competition in his school. Even singing contests, never mind that my dad could hold a tune like a sieve can hold water.

When he was twenty, he found a job as a cashier in a big, nationalized bank. The yearning in his heart to be excellent would take him from that entry-level job to a very influential position in the thirty odd years he worked in the bank. A few years in, when he was thirty-seven, he lost his wife. His life threatened to unravel, and he had to work hard to keep it together. He dealt with his dazed and grieving little kids - me and my older brother. He managed a million money problems we faced. All the while, the fire inside him to improve himself didn't diminish. He continued learning and trying new things.

He would wake up at four in the morning and write poems in Tamil, and essays in English. He would read books, lots of them. Striving was my dad's constant condition. He strived to better himself every day. He strived to have more influence in his bank. He strived to raise kids to be learned, talented, respected, and successful.

My dad was my first love and my first role model. I fashioned a lot of my personality after his. He gave me an insatiable love for learning. He taught me that one can never put a price on education. Growing up, even though we lived in cramped, dusty apartments and spent money with great care, my dad never scrimped on our learning. If I needed anything for my schoolwork – books, notebooks, pencils, erasers, binders, anything at all - I just had to ask. It didn't matter how much it cost. Dad would find the money for it.

He also taught me to go after what I wanted with courage, and to never shut down an option for the wrong reasons. I remember times when I would be ready to shut an option down because it involved working up the courage to ask someone something, or I lacked the confidence to see it through. "What is the worst that could happen if you go for it?" he would ask. "You ask for something and someone might say no. You try something and it might not succeed. So what? Just brush it off and move on to the next option."

But the most repeated lesson he taught me was to set my sights high. He wanted me to be ambitious. He was a striver in life, and he wanted me and my brother to be strivers too. To my father, ambition in life is as essential as breathing and blinking.

But is my dad right? Do we stop living once we stop striving?

Let me give you a contrasting example from my family.

One of my father's cousins – the son of the patriarch uncle of my father – is the opposite of us when it comes to career ambition. Like my father, this uncle found a job as a teller in a bank when he was in his twenties. But unlike my father, he decided early on that ambition was not for him. He didn't want to be buffeted from one town to the next, which was *de rigueur* in a bank job. So, he wrote a letter to his superiors stating that he didn't want to move out of Kumbakonam, and he didn't want to get promoted. It was a fair deal to make - "keep me here, even if it means you don't promote me". When he retired, my uncle was just slightly above the rank of a cashier.

My uncle is not unhappy, as far as I know. I did not know him to be unhappy when I lived in his house briefly during high school. He was contented, peaceful. His life took a different trajectory than my dad's, for sure. It was not marked by the insatiable ambition that was ever-present in my dad's life. He didn't have quite the same social capital as my father did over the years. He didn't touch the lives of as many people. But he didn't make the personal sacrifices that my dad had to make for his job. He raised a lovely, affectionate, happy, and well-functioning daughter. He saved enough money for his retirement. He lived an unexciting but peaceful life, and he continues to live quietly in the same town with his wife.

So, what is the best way to live? Should you constantly strive and set newer and bigger goals for yourself, like my dad did? Or should you search for peace and try to be satisfied with what you have?

I have come to the realization that, while it's hard to resist the need for a clear answer, it is not a one-size-fits-all. I am very much my father's daughter in this. I continue to strive and push in my life, even if it means constantly facing the demon of dissatisfaction. Ambition, while not recognized as such, especially in women, can be a good thing. Do not let anyone tell you otherwise. We aspire to do hard things, not easy things. We want to solve society's big problems. Once we shot for the moon and worked diligently toward getting there, planting those small steps for one but giant leaps for all. We dreamed of days when all humans could be truly treated as equals and marched relentlessly for it. On the flip side, being contented can be a profound well of personal peace. You can lead a more centered, happier life choosing this path.

Finding whether you want one or the other requires inner work. You, like my father, can repeatedly set and pursue goals, even if it means constantly facing the demon of dissatisfaction. Knowing the terrain of your journey - that being let down by success is inevitable - is great knowledge to have. But you can, with equal validity, choose contentment like my uncle did. You can be content with one aspect of your life – say, your personal records in golf – but ambitious in another – say, in your singing. You can also be contented at one stage in your life and build a furious fire within at another stage.

The key is to reflect often on what kind of life you want to live from here on out. Think about what will give you joy. Once you find that answer in your heart, accept the consequences - emotional and material - of it. Do not worry about what others are doing or saying. Regardless of your gender/race/sexual orientation, you can have a great life being ambitious. Just as equally, you can do the opposite. Do not compare yourself with others. Your choice is just as good as theirs. Make that choice intentionally, make it as often as needed, and do not let the currents of life carry you hither and thither.

Some parting thoughts

There is nothing wrong with being ambitious. In fact, ambition is great regardless of your race, gender, sexual orientation, or your background.

There is also nothing wrong with being content with your station in life.

You can be ambitious about some things in life, and chill about others. Reflect often on what kind of life you want to live and intentionally craft that life.

25

A Grand Life

How to craft a fulfilling life while having an illustrious career

I spent the last few days of 2020 in reflection and quiet work. The days were aimless and rainy, with dark clouds brooding over a slate-gray sky.

I did very few things in those silent, languid days. I ate a lot of sweet things, of course. Panettones and Stollen and Christmas cookies. I read a ton, and I wrote. But I also took the time to make a slide deck for an upcoming talk. I had been asked to give a talk on building a fulfilling life while having a career one can enjoy. What better way to write this talk - I thought - than to reflect on my own life and lessons? I opened my journal and started writing longform. I scribbled a list, titling it "My Rules". These are my mantras, my mottos, my principles.

These are truths that help me have a fulfilling, grand life. These are phrases I need to remind myself of often since I tend to forget them.

These are my truths, based on my predilections and faults. Perhaps some of these are yours too.

CHOOSE WHAT YOU CARE ABOUT.

Have you read this wonderful book "The Subtle Art of Not Giving a F*ck?" No, don't be turned off by its title. The book is not an argument for utter thoughtlessness about everything in your life. There are undoubtedly things that you should care about. For me - as 2020 made abundantly clear - these are my health, my significant relationships, and doing good work that matters. But we tend to care about too many things around us, and that's what the book preaches against.

Over the course of my life, I have learned to become choosier in this regard. I have learned to ask questions like: Does it really matter if a random co-worker doesn't like me? Why should I care what my aunt thinks about my life choices? Choose what you spend your mental calories on - it can free your mind.

MASTERY IS A PROCESS, NOT A STATE.

Many of us are in high-octane professions or have bold goals. Our work typically calls for a level of excellence that we are not born with. Becoming great at work will take time.

My first few years at Microsoft, as I told you in an earlier chapter, were painful. I felt so out of place in my team, like a polar bear in the Savannahs, that once I burst into tears while I was driving back home from home. Often, I would work on my code for several days and send my work to my team for feedback before checking it in to our source code repository. I would wait for an approval from a peer, perhaps a handful of comments to change a few things here and there. I routinely got back dozens of critiques from my colleagues.

Now, there are biases within the tech industry that causes requests for reviews sent by women developers to be judged more harshly than those by men developers. And of course, these critical reviews were soul-crushing, a beating to my ego. But I realized that there was truth in them too. More importantly, there was opportunity for me. I used every one of those code reviews as an opportunity to learn. To become a good developer, and then an excellent developer.

This process of "noticing my gaps -> learning -> getting feedback" is cyclical and has been ever-present in my career. Whether it is coding or leadership or speaking or writing, being at peace with not being an instant virtuoso has helped ease my mind.

TRUST THAT YOU WILL FIGURE IT OUT.

Think of the times you did something you thought impossible or tough at some point. I wrote about my cycling the Pacific Coast in an earlier chapter. That was one such thing for me. Another time, I decided to walk the Swiss Alps, from Chamonix to Zermatt, along a well-known path called the Haute Route. It took me about two weeks to walk the entire 100+ miles, scaling multiple passes. It was one of most wondrous things I have ever done. Night skies strewn with a million stars, massive blue glaciers tumbled over mountainsides, rumbling waterfalls, forests thick with trees, and winds so strong they could push you down if you don't take care. The walk was also one of the most challenging things I have done, completely beyond my comfort zone.

Just like the time I pedaled along the Pacific Coast, I was beset by doubts when I set out on the trek. There were many particularly dreadful sections, goat paths winding up mountains that felt like sheer heaps of rocks. With every step I took, my feet sank and slithered. But I did it, despite my self-doubts and fears. I watched where I planted my feet. I used rocks as leverage to pull myself up. It was slow going and nerve-wracking, but I figured it out.

It is the same deal with work. To do big, scary things - in life or work - you need to know deep down that you will figure it out. Because you will.

EVERY ENDEAVOR CAN TEACH YOU SOMETHING. BE CURIOUS.

It takes little experiments and baby steps to build that trust in yourself. When we build software products, in my team, we experiment a lot. We make little hypotheses and test them out. We learn. That is how we know when to build on and what to alter. Likewise, think of every activity you pursue - every interaction you have, every meeting you attend - as a little experiment that can help you learn something.

One of my mentors told me once to "collect data with every interaction". Approach your work with that scientist-like mindset and you will find that you look forward to many previously frightful activities.

DO NOT DWELL.

In 2018, I was asked to demo a few Microsoft technologies to a packed arena of IT Professionals. I had never done anything like that before, and understandably, I was nervous. My demo was 30 minutes long, split into two segments. I was in the middle of my second segment when I realized something was wrong with my demo. My prepared words were spilling out of my mouth, but what I expected on the screen didn't materialize. The product team had just deployed something that caused my script to become irrelevant. I stumbled.

Even today when I watch the video clip of it, I can see where I failed. When I got off the stage that day, feeling like a child who had just dropped her ice cream cone on dirt, I went straight to my team to say I was sorry. I had failed them. I had failed the demo. But my team didn't even notice my fumble. They thought everything had gone as planned. The moral: do not dwell on your screw-ups. Sure, failures are important learning opportunities, but there is no use in dwelling on what's happened. Besides, no one is intently watching everything you say and do. We are all too caught up in our own lives for that.

You have a right to a vision and voice of your own.

How many times do want to say something in a meeting, except you don't? You either feel nervous about opening your mouth or feel that your perspective is not that important. Know that your voice is important in your workplace. What's more, you have a right to be there, a right to voice your perspective, a vision that is all your own even if it is not the most popular one.

Do not take yourself too seriously.

Related to "do not dwell" is to loosen up. We are often very rigid in how we want people to view us. It is almost as though our self-esteem has gone on steroids and bulked up like the Hulk. We want everyone to think highly of us, to not laugh at us, ever. We want to hit a home run every time we come up to the plate. We inflate the importance of everything we do and of ourselves. We become stuffy, serious, and altogether no fun. Blunt words stab us like rapiers. Our ego becomes big, and our heart becomes small.

Listen to this story from author Elizabeth Gilbert. In her recent book *Big Magic*, Ms. Gilbert recounts a conversation she had with her neighbor Eileen once. Eileen loved to get tattoos on her body. When Gilbert asked her once how she could treat her body so casually with permanent ink, Eileen replied that it was only temporary. Gilbert understood Eileen's statement to mean that the tattoos were temporary. When she asked if all of them were temporary, Eileen replied, "No, Liz. My tattoos are permanent; it's my body that's temporary.

So is yours. We're here on earth only for a short while, so I decided a long time ago that I wanted to decorate myself as playfully as I can, while I still have time."

Ms. Gilbert and I have a love-hate relationship. Let me rephrase. I have a love-hate relationship with Ms. Gilbert. I love so much about her writing, and at the same time, I hate so much about it too. But I loved this part of Big Magic. Take a moment to let that sink in. *We are here on earth only for a short while.* So, what's the point of trying to be prissy, perfect, and important? Mess your hair up a bit and enjoy the lightness of being. That's how you can live a magical life.

DO YOUR WORK. THE OUTCOME AND PEOPLE'S REACTIONS ARE NOT YOUR CONCERN.

When I was growing up, my father often told me to do my best and leave the rest to God. In the Bhagavat Gita, Krishna advises Arjuna, "Do your duty; do not concern yourself with the outcome". In his memoir A Promised Land, Barack Obama talks about going into the Oval office every single day, reminding himself to "just do his job".

Non-attachment to the outcome can be a great thing. If you are trying to play the Beethoven's fifth symphony in an auditorium, spending your mental energies on how your music will sound to your audience, if the critics will praise you or flog you verbally, if your music career will take off or not, will not help one bit. You should just focus on the music and play.

In the world of your career, do your work and do not burden yourself with the outcome. What others think of what you do or say, whether they agree with it or not, whether it is well-received or not - these are not your concern. When you have to say something in a meeting, for example, do not agonize over what you have to say. Try to articulate to the best of your abilities, but do not tie yourself in knots or muzzle yourself because you worry about how you will sound to others.

I am not suggesting that you be abrasive, disrespectful, or callous of others' emotions. You should be empathetic, for sure, and phrase what you say effectively to not hurt or demean or exclude others. But focusing on your work - not on how it is going to be admired or reviled, how it is going to succeed or fail - can help you be happier and produce higher quality output.

MAKE TIME FOR IMPORTANT THINGS.

First, make a list of things that are important to you - work, health, relationships, fun. Anything else you're doing that doesn't contribute to what is important to you - like binge watching that show on Netflix, doomscrolling through Twitter, gossiping with a relative - cut it from your life. We often feel like we do not have time to do everything. Here is the thing: you don't need to do everything you're doing today. If you are intentional about where you're spending your time, you will magically mine minutes throughout the day that you can use for important things in your life.

IT'S OK TO BE IMPERFECT. IT MAKES YOU HUMAN.

A very good friend of mine, who is a master storyteller, makes her slides the morning of her talks. She hates rehearsing. I, on the other hand, overthink what I say and how I say it. I come from a long line of people who didn't like to "get laughed at" by their neighbors and family, so aiming for perfection is as easy as mixing salt and water for me. It is not just me, though. Many luminaries that I admire - from Melinda Gates to Angela Merkel to Michelle Obama - are famous over-preparers. Christine LaGarde, the president of European Central Bank once said this about her preparation.

When we work on a particular matter, we will work the file inside, outside, sideways, backwards, historically, genetically, and geographically. We want to be completely on top of everything, and we want to understand it all, and we don't want to be fooled by somebody else.

Financial Times, July 2019

I have nothing against preparation. I continue to be someone who likes to prepare, especially for important meetings and events. But I also know that overpreparing can kill your ability to think on your feet. More importantly, it can make you anxious and lose valuable time. In the world of software development, we say that Done is better than perfect. It is true for life too. Remember that you are only human, and people know that. Most people are not expecting perfection from you.

So those are some of my truths and reminders. Here is what I urge you to do. Take a notebook and a pen, reflect on your own experiences and tendencies, and make a list of your own truths. What are the things that you need to remind yourself of often? What are some tendencies that keep getting in your way? May be some of my truths are yours too and you are welcome to borrow my mantras. But do spend some quiet time reflecting about yourself and what a fulfilling life means to you.

Will you do it?

Some parting thoughts

Find yourself some quiet time. Reflect on your life, experiences, and lessons. Think of tendencies that impede your career. Make your empowering phrases or mantras for your life. These are your own rules that you will remind yourself of every day.

Choose what you care about.

Every endeavor can teach you something. Be curious.

Mastery is a process, not a state.

Trust that you got it in you to figure it out. Raise your hand despite your fears.

Do not dwell on failures.

Do your job. Do not focus on the outcome. People's reactions to your work are not your business.

Make time for things that are important to you.

It's ok to be imperfect. It makes you human. Do not fall prey to the Hydra of perfectionism.

26

On the margins

Lifting others up as you succeed

Their names were Yasmin and Fatima. Yasmin, the eldest, was fifteen years old. Fatima was fourteen. Their parents had rented a place out to my dad when he lived in a town called Salem. I was living with my uncle and aunt at the time, and I visited Salem for the first time during my summer break of 1992, which was when I first met Yasmin and Fatima.

The girls fascinated me. They had delicate skin, skin that turned pink like rose milk in the blistering Indian heat. They had lush curly hair and brilliant irises flecked with chestnut brown. They were self-assured, rich, elegant, and beautiful. I was slightly intimidated by them.

One day, I worked up the courage to talk to them. We quickly became friends. I spent many afternoons in their warm company. They told me all about the local customs. They shared neighborhood gossip, complained about their parents, and talked about boys. We ate roasted peanuts from paper cones, sitting with our legs folded beneath us. I was thrilled that they chose to be my friends, that they chose to share their stories with me. As the time came for me to leave Salem, I started feeling a pang in my heart. I knew I'd miss Yasmin and Fatima.

A few days before I left, Fatima found me, alone on our common terrace, gathering the crackling hot clothes that had dried on our clothesline.

"My sister is getting married," she said without much ado.

I looked at her, confused. Yasmin was just 15-years old, a high schooler like me. How could she get married off so young? Fatima didn't feel anything odd about the arrangement. She had come there to just tell me the news, not to bemoan what was happening.

Later, my dad told me that it was not uncommon for "girls like Fatima and Yasmin" to get married before they finished high school. By that he meant girls in small towns, girls with parents that kept the old ways of old religions, girls with parents that were not very educated themselves. In the case of Yasmin, her family just wanted her married before she became "unmarketable". Older, more educated girls were deemed more trouble, and therefore less desirable. To them, a woman who worked not just took away a job that was rightfully a man's, but her character could be thrown into question too.

In the end, I didn't attend Yasmin's wedding. I had to leave Salem before then. But my dad told me that the wedding was a lavish affair. Yasmin sparkled with rows of gold necklaces around her neck. Over a thousand guests attended. Yasmin dropped out of school and was misty-eyed when she left her father's home, but she was happy. She had achieved one of the biggest goals that she had been trained to pursue: make yourself attractive enough for someone of good status to marry you. Yasmin and Fatima weren't encouraged to have dreams beyond that. Most of their lives, their work would be the traditional kind of a woman: the work of a mother, the work of a homemaker, the work of a caretaker for the elderly.

It was not just Yasmin that left me with the nagging question, "But what about school?"

Before I was five, my mother had the habit of leaving me in the care of our helper Meenakshi. Meenakshi was a skinny woman with a face that was shriveled like a dark raisin. She lived in a shanty by a canal filled with flotsam, and she took me there with her often. Her house had one room where her family slept, cooked, and bathed. I spent many an afternoon in her home, wrapped in the smells of onions and old oil. Meenakshi became like a mother to me. She often fed me Tamarind rice from her aluminum plate, mixing a spicy and tangy homemade paste with cold rice. She was a poor woman with a heart as large as the ocean.

Meenakshi had a 10-year daughter Lalli who played with me and told me stories while her mother cooked. Lalli never went to school, would never go to school in her life. Sometimes she would run her hands over my schoolbooks wrapped in crisp, brown paper, and take a whiff of their insides, but she could not read what was written in them. When Lalli was fifteen, she was sent off to be the live-in help for someone in Delhi. I never thought of it then, but have frequently done so after: How could someone like Lalli escape the life she found herself in? How could she become someone who could go to school and then college and then off to a job that would pay her well?

I was undoubtedly more privileged than Lalli. I was born into more money than her, a more dominant caste than her, to parents with more education than hers. But I had my struggles too. My folks liked to stay true to the old ways, and I had to argue for the many things that I wanted to do: to study, to study further, to have a career, and so on. In my family, women were always an afterthought. We ate after all the menfolk had finished eating. I washed my brother's and my dad's dinnerplates, clattering them over our sink. My brother was expected to do his homework in the evenings, whereas I was expected to help around the house - and only after that, do my homework. In college, I was told that I was wasting a "seat" that a boy deserved more.

But still, I had my guardian angels. My dad believed in my right to an education. He believed that I could make something of myself, besides being a mother and a wife. He stood by my side against everyone who questioned my right to be "so studious". My aunt Sundari inspired me to pursue a career. We could afford books, notebooks, pens, and uniforms.

Lalli had none of that. Her family expected her to bring in money when she was just a child, not spend it on school and books. I could see how people like Lalli - marginalized, mistreated, abandoned by society - could find it hard to escape the vortex they were in. I could see how people like Yasmin didn't have role models of career women, or even people around them that encouraged them to pursue a career.

I have lost touch with Lalli, Yasmin, and Fatima. Meenakshi is now dead. After I became a leader at Microsoft, in a media interview, someone asked me why I felt so strongly about inclusion of marginalized people in our workplace. Here is why:

Because I know that including everyone's potential in our workplace will make for more innovation and better products.

Because I know that it is better for our economy to not leave hordes of people and their productivity out.

Because I know that the world will be a better place to have everyone lifted.

Because I know tech education empowers people, and empowered people can make big things happen for humanity.

But more than any of that...I feel, in my bones, the struggles that people on the margins face. Girls that must defeat not just the voices of society, but their own inner voices, to be successful in male-dominated fields. Children that do not have the luxury of playing on their Xboxes or even using a computer in the evenings. Children that must work to fund not just their education, but that of their siblings too. Girls that are expected to get married when they are barely adults, and if they become professionals at all, it must have been after many pitched battles. Women like my own mother-in-law who, even though she was bringing in her fair share of her family's income, was expected to do 100% of the unpaid labor at home too.

I know about the odds stacked against people like them, the people on the margins of our world. I know it is the morally right thing to do, to empower folks on the margins and make sure they have a seat at the table. One of the best humans that ever walked this earth, Justice Ruth Bader Ginsburg, famously said this, and like many things she said, it makes a lot of sense.

"I tell law students...if you want to be a true professional, you will do something outside yourself... something that makes life a little better for people less fortunate than you."

People with privilege have a responsibility to help pull up a stepstool for the less privileged folks to stand on. I have been advised many times by well-wishers not to take up the cause of women or other marginalized people. This advice often comes from a good place. My people don't want me to suffer any adverse consequences at work because of any kind of crusade I might send myself on. But this is a cause that is important. Important to all of us because of all the reasons above, and important to me deeply, because of who I am, where I come from, and everything that has made me. If you feel strongly about this – and I believe you should – do not fear to take up this cause. Lifting another up as you soldier on yourself will make you feel more empowered, and it will empower the other person too. It is a win from all angles.

Some parting thoughts

Go the extra mile to include and empower the people on the margins in your life.

There are so many people around the world – the poor, women in oppressive societies, people of color – that face many hurdles on their way to success. If they become professionals at all, it likely would have involved several struggles. Be mindful of that in your workplace. Do not expect perfection, especially in interview loops.

Be empathetic and inclusive. Try to learn people's stories and connect.

When you are successful, lift others up.

27

Frequently Asked Questions

I am a developer and a woman, and I don't feel like I belong here.
Should I become a Program Manager or move to the Marketing or
Human Resources department?

I get it. Being a woman in tech is not easy. It is tempting to call it quits
and do something else. But believe me, you are in the right place. As
technologists, and especially women developers, we have a superpower.
We are robins among ravens. We are different, we are remarkable, we have
real skills with our own unique twists, and we stand out. All of these can
certainly be detractors in our career, but they are also what gives us strength.

As a woman, you bring different qualities to the table that are perhaps
absent in your team. Leverage those differences for your own progress. You
can make a difference to your team and to yourself. It is better to be in a place
where you are unique as opposed to where you are one in a hundred.

This book is full of lessons and advice to help you navigate your place in
your team as a minority. Give these tips a try. Recruit allies and your own
power tribe – your squad of people that support you in your inner power. If,
after giving it a shot for a few months, maybe a few years, you still feel rotten
about being a developer, then – and only then – pivot.

How did you decide to become a manager? How do I know if I should
become a manager of people?

I became a manager because an opportunity became available to fill an important gap in my team. When I was offered it, I didn't know much about people management. I took it because I like to try new things and build new knowledge. People management is one such area I wanted to learn about. I love the challenge of understanding humans: what kicks us into high gear, what drags us down, what inspires us, and so on. I also knew that, if I failed at people management or didn't like it, I could always go back to being a developer. Remember: most decisions in life are reversible. So, I raised my hand to do it, and I have been a manager now for many years.

How do you know if you should make the leap? Refer to the chapter "First impressions on the job", where I talk about how to decide if you should change to a different team. A lot of that discussion applies to this question too. You want to be deliberate about your decision, but also know that it is not life-and-death. Give yourself that gift of lightness of being.

Being a manager or being an individual contributor on your team are both equally viable and valid choices. No matter what you choose, do you work with passion, gain mastery, and bring value. That, as you now know, is how you can be successful.

I am not very good at Networking, but I hear I need to do it. How
can I make it easier for myself?

A lot of us are introverts, and we love socializing with strangers as much as a malamute loves to take baths. Networking, especially, has a bad rap. You go to a social event where you hardly know anyone, make small talk, eat potato chips and popcorn, and simper and smile. All the while, your feet hurt, and you are thinking about going home and reading your book and listening to the hum of your refrigerator. How can you make this whole exercise more pleasant?

Think of networking as conversations where you are collecting data from various people. You want to give people an opportunity to talk about themselves. You want to hear their story out, know more about their lives and their work. People love talking about themselves and they will talk when invited. Have some questions handy to strike up a conversation: what is your day like at this job? What do you like about this company? If you had no worries about anything, what would you do for work? What excites you about this field? These questions can shine a light on their current workplace but also on the human being you're talking to. Be ok with whitespaces and awkward silences. Listen and store away the tidbits in your head.

Above all, try not to take yourself too seriously, and try to have fun.

How can I get my voice heard in a meeting, when I am usually so quiet and people tend to talk over me?

Let me tell you about someone I work with at Microsoft. We shall call her Juliette. She is a Program Manager (PM) at the company, and she and I were in a meeting together recently. The room was full of people, about thirty engineers and PMs and managers. The topic of conversation got heated at one point and everyone started talking over one another. It was at this moment that I saw Juliette did something I admired.

She got up unannounced. Every face in the room swiveled to look at her. Everyone, including me, wondered what she was doing standing up in the middle of the meeting. She remained silent for a minute, and then clearly said, "I know we all have opinions on this. But now we are going to listen to David, and then we are going to move on so we can talk about other topics."

That's it. The room went quiet. David spoke, and we moved on.

Juliette did two things there that impressed me. One: she got up, making herself physically dominant. Juliette is a small woman and by standing up, she made herself physically more noticeable. It was also an unexpected gesture, so everyone waited to see what she would do next. Two: she clearly stated the ground rules. That we are going to give someone the floor and then stop belaboring.

Now, you can dissect what Juliette did there in both positive and negative ways. Was it right for Juliette to shut down the raucous conversation and silence many people in the room? Was it her place to hit the reset button and lay out the ground rules for the meeting? Isn't it odd that someone needs to be physically assertive to get heard in a meeting? All fair questions. Regardless, Juliette showed leadership that day and showed me one way in which you can get heard amidst cacophony.

Juliette also showed us that we should say what we have to say clearly, calmly, and without droning on or mumbling. These are mistakes that I have seen many people make. Even if you don't say a lot in the meeting and you're not the loudest voice in the room, how you say the things you say matters. If you believe in what you're saying, make sure that comes across. It's important not to sound tentative. Read the chapter on the art of storytelling and the chapter on writing. The advice there can help you articulate your points succinctly and effectively in meetings as well.

How can you influence decisions when people making decisions are
more senior than you?

Your first job is to think about it from your senior leader's perspective. What do they want? Most people working for corporations want to be successful in what they do. And they can be successful if they make the best decisions possible. How can you help them make the best decisions? What data can you present and how can you pitch your ideas to them, so they can be persuaded toward specific actions?

Senior leaders responsible for making decisions are generally looking for credibility in what you are pitching. Therefore, when you pitch an idea to senior people, show them that you've thought through it and it's going to make the business successful or make them as individuals successful. Use the ideas outlined in the chapter about storytelling to capture their attention and land your pitch well.

To pitch your ideas, you can have one-on-ones with people that have the authority to make changes. Alternatively, you can find the influencers of this person with authority and pitch to them. You can prototype your idea and show proof to the team that the idea has legs. Often an idea in action, a concrete prototype, has a better chance of convincing people than an abstract promise. You can write up a white paper or a document about your idea and socialize the document with the stakeholders in the team.

These are all the many ways to have influence in your team when you are not the ultimate decision-maker. May be one of these will work for you, or perhaps you should try more than one approach simultaneously.

```
I don't think this work gives me meaning. How do I find out what
is my calling?
```

A calling, in my opinion, is overrated. If you set out on a quest to find your calling, you can travel a long, arduous, and often disenchanting path. Instead find meaning in what you do right now. Most work we do has meaning. It is up to us to find it.

Are you working on testing software in a consultancy company that takes on disconnected projects from different clients? Think about how your work testing code will help the developer who wrote that code produce better quality products. Think about the end users who will use that product enjoying a less defective experience. Understand who the customers for your work are and how you are benefiting them.

Are you working as an Operations engineer for a company that produces online services? Think about how your work deploying bits to production helps save time for the many software engineers in your company. Think about how your constant vigilance helps keep critical services running for the customers of those services.

If, after doing a lot of introspection on how exactly your current work helps the world, you still find your job meaningless, find another job if you can afford to. But this time, as you look for your next job, make sure you understand how it can give you meaning in your life.

How can I be more productive? How can I do more in my life with such little time?

The question of work-life balance is ubiquitous. First, I have to say, I have been fortunate in life - and have made life choices - that help me have more time on my hands. For example, I have a husband that shoulders the household burden equally with me. I do not have dependents – elderly people that need care or kids - at home. I have worked toward a level of economic independence that will allow me to delegate the most tedious, unexciting, unimportant chores to people I can hire.

I know that not everyone has the inclination or the privilege to make those choices. But if you can, do so. Having equal partnership at home can be the biggest advantage one has in their career. If you do not have it, feel empowered to ask for it. Have conversations with your partner where you assert what you're asking for, and why it is important to you. If you can hire people to clean your house, if you can get your groceries delivered to you, do so. Delegate as many unimportant tasks as possible.

Make an inventory of all the other activities that take up your time. Watching episode after episode of that detective series on Netflix goes in there. Reading to your child goes in there. Doomscrolling on Twitter goes in there. Going for a run goes in there. Now look at the list and reclaim the time spent on activities that do not help you in any way, activities that leave you feeling numb or even more bored at the end of them.

I love integrating my life with my work. My company gives me the flexibility to do so. I can schedule a one hour walk on my calendar in the middle of the day, and no one cares as long as I get my work done. Likewise, I sometimes work for hours after dinner, and no one at home is much bothered by it. I also know of colleagues who like more airtight compartments for work and life. They don't want work to seep into life-time, and life to seep into work-time. There is no silver bullet here. Do what feels right for you but be intentional about the time you are spending on mindless things.

133

What is the Number 1 skill or quality that has helped you in your career growth at Microsoft?

This question is hard for many reasons. I cannot point to just one thing that has helped me in my career. Having access to opportunities and great managers has helped greatly, for sure, but so has my hard work and my ability to learn new things. But if you put a gun to my head (and I really hope you don't) and ask me to name just ONE thing, I'd say it is the energy I put into processing and responding to feedback.

People say that feedback is a gift, and when they do, it sounds like one of those boring clichés. But indeed, feedback is something that you should cherish, especially when it comes from people that you trust and respect. Whether it's feedback on your code or your document or yourself, learn to respond and not simply react. When the feedback is critical of you, there is no denying that it hurts the moment you receive it. But learn to sift the grain from the chaff. Learn to put aside your own emotional reaction to it (after letting your emotions course through your system), and to act on the facts hidden within it. Make a plan to become better. Act on the plan. Show to the people that gave you that feedback that you're better thanks to the feedback they gave you. The people closest to me can tell you that I do "react" to feedback now and then, but I have learned to give myself the gift of time to reflect and process it better. That, I think, is something that can help anyone grow leaps and bounds.

I am a senior developer, in a new role that has me working more with people and less with code. I am getting frustrated - not sure if I am making any progress with all these meetings and collaboration. Did you feel this way when you switched from an individual contributor to a lead? How did you cope with it?

The instant gratification you get from seeing your code work on the screen is powerful, like a drug indeed. To this day, I find that joy unparalleled. When I started working more primarily on leadership roles, and less on coding deliverables, I did miss that satisfaction quite a bit. Working with people can be frustrating, especially in the early days of people leadership. Enabling people to be productive, helping them grow, can take a long time to show results. Bye-bye instant gratification!

As I started to understand my role as a leader, I realized that I actually didn't have much of a clue how to do it right. Unlike coding, they did not teach me "people skills" in college. Leading people was a skill that I sorely needed to learn. So, I reframed my thought that "working with people is frustrating and less fun than coding" to "I need to become better at working with people". I had to learn to "debug people" like I knew how to debug code. This quest to learn something new was a challenge. The challenge excited me, and that excitement overcame my feeling of frustration.

The leadership training that Microsoft put me through as a new leader helped a lot. I learned about the SCARF model that unpacked the social motivations of people. I sought out books that helped me understand human behavior better. Some books I recommend include Emotional Intelligence by Dan Goleman, The five dysfunctions of a team by Patrick Lencioni, Thinking Fast and Slow by Daniel Kahneman, and Flow by Mihaly Csikszentmihalyi.

Will shifting your focus to people mean you won't have quite so much time to code anymore? The sad truth is, yes, all of this takes time and there are only so many hours in your workday. Some people I know fill in the gap by using personal time in the evening to code. I used to do that more before I decided to branch out into other "side hustles". But do keep in mind that understanding people better and building those relationships are not wasted endeavors. It is time well spent and will pay off many times over as you progress in your career.

```
I recently became an engineering manager, and have been successful
in my career so far. Should I do anything different to continue to
be successful from here on out?
```

The other day, I saw a book in the library titled "What got you here won't get you there". I didn't check out the book and read it. But I do agree with the title. The skills that helped you succeed early in your career are different from the ones you'll need as you become increasingly senior. Here are some skills that I have found are important to sharpen in the more senior ranks:

Business acumen: Understand how your business works, what your market looks like, how you can impact the bottom line, what new strategy you need to develop, and how you can grow the pie. Constantly innovate, and constantly look for opportunities.

Communication: At a certain level of seniority, technical excellence becomes table stakes. Every one of your peers is likely proficient in writing/testing code or defining products (or whatever else you do). What becomes crucial in differentiating you is your ability to articulate. There are three situations in which you need to master communication. I have touched upon some of these ideas in earlier chapters about meetings, storytelling, and writing.

Landing your ideas in meetings. You'll be in many meetings where you must inform, persuade, or influence people. You need to be able to capture the attention of the room and articulate your ideas clearly and concisely. This is an art that needs a lot of practice. A tool I gave my mentee is to structure her ideas in her head in numbered lists. For example: "There are two options here for us. They are 1)...and 2)...", "There are three things I want to talk about today. 1)...2)...3)...", "There were four steps to this process", etc. A caveat is to not have a list with fifteen items - no one will remember it, including yourself.

Public speaking and writing. Have a platform to speak about the product you're building, your cultural values, and your ideas. Cultivate a writing habit - whether it is in the form of documents or emails to your team or blog posts. Lack of clear big-picture communication often is a detractor for team satisfaction. Seek out speaking and presentation opportunities and practice your public speaking skills.

"Crucial conversations". These are conversations - with your peers, your team, your stakeholders, your customers - that require diplomacy and nuance. You need to learn to be empathetic while delivering success and showing authenticity at the same time. You need to learn to be agile, not just to think on your feet, but to correct when things go awry. Of course, there are very few people I know that are masters at this, and it is a hard skill to learn. You can learn it by reading some of the books I recommended earlier, but there is no replacement for practicing it intentionally in your own tough conversations.

Bold decision making: When I was a junior engineer, one of my managers told me that my growth would be limited by my lack of appetite for risk-taking. A lot of us that do not come from a position of privilege tend to naturally shy away from risks. We worked hard to get here, and we don't want to squander it all away by sticking our necks out. But being brave and taking some calculated risks, I have found, are essential for progress. Use data to drive your decisions, but do not get paralyzed in analysis. Give yourself permission to fail, to be rejected, to be not perfect. Doing that helped me a great deal.

Everybody says we need mentors for professional success. Is that true? If so, how can approach someone to be my mentor and keep the connection alive?

I have found that mentorship helps enormously. I learn a lot from what my mentors teach me, and who they are. They coach me, they care for my success, and they role model good leadership. But how do I find my ideal mentor?

First off, I don't believe in one ideal mentor. You need a board of mentors. People that you look up to for various aspects of your work and life. Some of these mentors will challenge you and critique you, and some will cheer you on and inspire you. Assemble your board carefully and with intention.

When you approach someone for mentorship, do a bit of research on them. If they are someone you know very well, someone you have worked with, then this becomes easier. This is how I have personally found my mentors. I usually reach out to folks in my professional circle whom I respect and admire.

But if you are approaching someone you heard give a talk once, go to them with some background information. You might say to them something like, "I have followed your work here, here, and here. And I really appreciate what you said and have respect for your professional success. Your perspectives resonate a lot with me, and I would love to connect with you for occasional guidance. I am so and so, and I have been in this field for this long. I frequently get stuck in these places. Examples of questions I am struggling with right now are below. It would be a privilege if I could get 30 minutes of your time every quarter to chat. I understand if you do not have the time now and would love to keep in touch. But if you do have the time, I'd love to set up a meeting so I can properly introduce myself. Thank you."

Note that mentors typically agree to take on proteges not for any pointed benefit of their own. I have heard advice like "offer to give back something to your mentor", which I find a bit ludicrous. I know I derive a lot of personal value from mentoring others– including life satisfaction, getting grounded about what younger people are dealing with, expanded network, and so on – but I rarely think of the relationship as quid pro quo. Know that most seasoned people in later stages of their career are happy to give back and find satisfaction in it. So, approach them with confidence.

28

Conclusion

Since the days of our ancestors that shaved stones into weapons, we have passed on stories and learned from others' life experiences. I wrote this book because I wanted to pass on some of my lessons to you. I have presented the stories from my early life and my career as truthfully and transparently as I can, and as well as I can remember. Did I miss anything? Did I simplify some topics? Perhaps. But this is the advice you will hear from me if you were my mentee.

Technology is a place where we make things happen for the world. Increasingly, humans rely on technology for much of their life, work, and happiness. I cannot imagine being without the communication platforms that connect me with my family thousands of miles away. There is so much more access to resources now with the Internet, and so many more ways for us to be productive and entertained. Technology is the field of today and of tomorrow. It is a place where you would want to be, not just for impact to others but for impact to yourself too. It is no secret that folks employed in tech make good money.

With all that goodness come the challenges as well. Diversity in tech continues to be dismal. In most top tech companies, employees that identify themselves as women make up less than thirty-two percent of the workforce. This number shrinks drastically in technical roles, like software development, and as you look at higher ranks in the corporate hierarchy. The numbers are even more appalling for Hispanic and Black populations in tech. This is particularly harmful as we think about all the new things that are getting invented now and will become our way of life tomorrow. Artificial Intelligence and robots will need to be programmed and taught how to process the world. We want such autonomous systems to not have biases that arise from being the progeny of their largely homogenous creators. We want diversity in tech, now more than ever. This is how we can expect to create a more equitable and just future for humanity.

Companies like Microsoft believe in the value of Diversity and Inclusion. I have worked at Microsoft for over fifteen years now, and I know how this value animates every fiber of the company's being. Our leadership invests in this heavily and we are always thinking of ways to recruit, retain, and grow diverse talent. Every meeting room in Microsoft has a poster that lists the ten inclusive behaviors we should observe.

1. Include and seek input from people across a wide variety of backgrounds
2. Listen carefully to the person speaking until they feel understood
3. Make a habit of asking questions
4. If you have a strong reaction to someone, ask yourself why
5. Address misunderstandings and resolve disagreements
6. Act to reduce stressful situations
7. Understand each person's contribution
8. Examine your assumptions
9. Ensure all voices are heard
10. Be brave

Our senior people are trained on inclusive hiring, allyship, navigating through differences and other topics relevant to diversity. Leaders get rated on how they and their teams do with inclusion.

These are all wonderful. I support all these investments and appreciate that we are doing more and more in this regard. But despite all these efforts undertaken by many companies in the industry, underrepresented folks continue to face an uphill battle in their trek to the upper echelons of the corporate ladder. Some of these struggles arise from company cultures not changing to become more inclusive, despite good intentions and sponsorship from leadership. Some come from unconscious biases all of us hold. We must continue to speak up and shine light on areas where culture can be improved.

But some of these struggles are individual. Across the industry, I hear from people from underrepresented backgrounds that need support and guidance in navigating their own personal obstacles and career questions. It is for that reason I wrote this book. I was once that scared newcomer in this field, dealing with my own impediments, and feeling lost about how I could succeed in a place full of people that looked nothing like me. I learned several lessons that helped, and I continue to learn more. I want to share those lessons with the hope that you'll find them useful in your own career.

To recap, here are some of those lessons that I have shared in this book.

Do not shy away from speaking up, asserting your rights, or sharing your perspective.

Watch, learn, adapt, and reinvent yourself often.

You deserve a career and to stand on your own legs.

Lift others behind you.

Be intentional about your ambitions, and how you want to lead your life.

Failures can fuel success. Rejections do not portend permanent misery.

Embrace the unknown and raise your hand for bold, epic opportunities.

Communicating well – whether it is through speaking or writing – is a key skill for your tech career. Practice and master that skill.

Be audacious. Take some risks with the projects you sign up for.

A lot of us constantly compare ourselves to others. This often comes from how we have been educated. The "star pupil syndrome" can hurt your emotional well-being and can affect your work, so it is best to stop being victim to it.

Learn to deal with your negative self-talk. One of the most effective ways I have found is to develop your own mental mantras.

You have a right to your voice and perspectives. Voice them, but voice them well.

Sift through the stories you tell yourself. Deal with them with mindful-

ness.

Choose what you care about. Do not concern yourself with other people's reactions.

Do not dwell on your screw-ups. Learn from your failures.

Make time for important things.

Career success has four components: passion, excellence, impact, and exposure.

I have had my turbulent times and my quiet times in both my life and work. I have had my ups and downs, and I have survived. I was once a scared lonely girl from a small South Indian town, who started her life with little English, little money, few connections, and many societal biases against her. I found my way to success in tech. If I can do that, so can you. I have shared my stories with the hope of showing you glimpses of my past and sharing a few practical things I have learned. Hope you find these lessons and tips valuable. I have enjoyed writing this book, and I hope you have enjoyed reading it too.

29

Acknowledgments

How often do you read the Acknowledgments section of a book? If you are like me, not very often. So, I promise to keep this short.

Of course, I cannot begin anything in my life without a thought or two of gratitude toward my dear father, V. Rajagopalan. He raised me with an unbelievable amount of love, concern, and care. Despite his old-fashioned upbringing and his complex personality, he believed that girls should be educated as much as boys. He encouraged me in all competitive and intellectual endeavors. He sacrificed so much for me, and he continues to be my biggest fan. I cannot repay my debt to you, ever, dad.

My dear husband, Narayan Krishnamoorthy, is not just my supporter and cheerleader, he is also the first person that reads anything I write for publishing. When I got promoted to Partner level at Microsoft, some folks congratulated me for not just a job well done, but also for having such a wonderful partner that supports me like no other. This is indeed true. Indra Nooyi, the ex-CEO of PepsiCo, often says that marrying the right guy was her first key to success. In my case, I am so fortunate that I found this key early in life. I am deeply grateful to Narayan for everything he does for me: stocking our pantry every week, taking the garbage out, doing our laundry, putting up with my bad jokes, taking care of me when I am sick, but most importantly...being my sounding board, the shoulder I cry on, and the person that often witnesses the rawest forms of my anxieties. Thank you, my love.

I am thankful to everyone at work that taught me something and made me better. My mentors, my sponsors, my supporters, my advisors, my work-friends. Thank you for believing in me and my work, constantly pushing me to be better, and for giving me wings to fly.

30

Resources

Books on storytelling
Spin your tale, Dona Sarkar, https://www.amazon.com/Spin-Your-Tale-Fiction-Personal/dp/1725879913

Made to stick, Chip and Dan Heath, https://www.amazon.com/Made-Stick-Ideas-Survive-Others/dp/1400064287

Talk like TED, Carmine Gallo, https://www.amazon.com/Talk-Like-TED-Carmine-Gallo-audiobook/dp/B00H4D8OLS

Books to learn mindfulness
The Headspace guide to meditation, Andy Puddicombe, https://www.amazon.com/Headspace-Guide-Meditation-Mindfulness-Minutes/dp/B0088UU8R4

10% happier, Dan Harris, https://www.amazon.com/dp/B07PQT9LWQ

Books to learn more on the topic of people of the margins
Half the sky, Nicholas Kristof, https://www.goodreads.com/book/show/6260997-half-the-sky

The moment of lift, Melinda Gates, https://www.goodreads.com/book/show/40776644-the-moment-of-lift

Behind the beautiful forevers, Katherine Boo, https://www.goodreads.com/book/show/11869272-behind-the-beautiful-forevers

About the Author

In her day job, Raji Rajagopalan is a Partner Director of Software Engineering at a Fortune 50 company. Her journey in tech started two decades ago, working for a firmware company in Canada. Her work has spanned building startups, growing global teams, and creating products used by more than a billion customers. She has worked with over fifty entrepreneurs to bootstrap their own social enterprises. As a leader, her mission is to build diverse, innovative teams that do outstanding work, where every employee feels like they belong and can make a difference in their own lives and in the world.

Raji mentors young professionals and sponsors many Diversity and Inclusion efforts in her organization. She has run large teams of software engineers across five countries and four continents. She is often called an inspiration and a role model to underrepresented professionals and immigrants, especially women of color. She is regularly invited to speak at conferences globally on topics ranging from technology to women's issues to career progression.

Raji has published her writing in magazines such as Herizons, India Currents, and Khabar, and she is a regular writer on her blog. In her spare time, Raji loves traveling, photography, and books. You can learn more about her on her website www.rajiraj.com.

Made in the USA
Monee, IL
19 January 2023

24724139R00085